Sin
Reconsidered

James Gaffney

To my friends
of IBC !

PAULIST PRESS
New York/Ramsey

Library of Congress
Catalog Card Number: 82-61424

ISBN: 0-8091-2516-1

Published by Paulist Press
545 Island Road, Ramsey, N.J. 07446

Printed and bound in the
United States of America

Contents

To Dad
who deserves a more jovial topic!

1
What Are They Saying About Sin?

To the question in this chapter's title one's first inclination may be to reply, "Curiously little." Indeed, when Karl Menninger, nearly a decade ago, entitled his book *Whatever Became of Sin?* he was echoing a not uncommon, though generally unspoken question. References to sin, which had lately seemed to occupy a very large and sometimes even predominant place in Christian religious discourse, had become in recent years relatively infrequent and, what is more significant, noticeably uneasy. This diminished and disconcerted attention to sin was discernible in popular religious writing, sermonizing, and catechetics. Moreover, within the Catholic Church a spectacular decline in recourse to the sacrament of penance, recently renamed reconciliation, bore witness to a widespread disinclination not only to discuss sin homiletically, but to confess it sacramentally. Ritual innovations for modernizing a penitential liturgy, although introduced with official solemnity and pastoral ingenuity, were received in most places with very limited interest. And as sin receded toward the periphery of popular religious attention, so also did traditional themes closely related to sin, such as temptation and concupiscence, purgatory and judgment, devils and hell.

Menninger raised his question from the advantageous point of view of a psychiatrist who had been for some time observing among his patients a progressive disregard of moral fault as a factor to be taken practical account of. Guilt they experienced plentifully. But they tended to regard guilt mainly as a malady of the mind, paying little or no attention to the possibility that it might in fact be a perfectly appropriate reaction to their real moral condition. Their problem, as they preceived it, was that they *felt* guilty. Whether or not, in some more objective sense, they might be guilty was not treated as a practical question. What they wanted, and would be satisfied to obtain, was release not from guilt, but from feeling guilty.

A few years after Menninger, another popular summons to reopen the books on sin was issued by Henry Fairlie's *The Seven Deadly Sins Today,* which is concerned to point out how inadequately the flaws and failures of life are dealt with once the idea of sin is banished from our thinking, and to demonstrate by contrast how applicable to our modern situation are ancient monastic categories of basic moral wrongness. Fairlie's recommendation is the more interesting inasmuch as he is—though, he notes, reluctantly—an unbeliever. He is thus an eloquent example of that not uncommon type of modern thinker who, while unable to adopt religion, finds himself unable to say certain things he needs to say without words and ideas borrowed from religious tradition.

It may seem paradoxical that some of the most notable recent discussions of sin have come from secular sources, while in the churches themselves the very idea of sin seems to be losing currency. Yet a full generation has passed since H. Richard Niebuhr summed up his sardonic history of American churchly ideology as a transformation of earlier conceptions of Christianity into *The Kingdom of God in America,* where, as he memorably expressed it, "a God without wrath brought men without sin into a kingdom without judgment through the ministrations of a Christ without a cross." When Niebuhr wrote those words he was applying them to that liberal Protestantism whose progressive acquiescence in secular predilections he so keenly observed. They could hardly have been applied with equal force to Roman Catholicism. Yet it would not be long before Catholic self-criticism sounded a note rather like Niebuhr's. The main thing that had happened to Roman Catholicism in the meanwhile was the Second Vatican Council.

There is no mistaking, in the records of that Council's properly theological debates, that the most insistent theme of serious misgiving about how things seemed to be going was a fear that religiously sanctioned humanism and optimism had, in consequence of over-eagerness to sound a distinctively positive and modern note, obscured, distorted, or trivialized authentically Christian views concerning evil in general and sin in particular. After the Council, and especially during the recent and still-rising tide of ultra-conservative and anti-conciliar Catholic reaction, similar concerns have been expressed by a large and growing minority. Thus far, however, none of this seems to have stimulated any major effort by Catholic theologians either to refashion a theology of sin along more severe and tragic lines, or to highlight the grimmer aspects of earlier teachings concerning sin.

Indeed, what "they"—meaning Roman Catholic theologians— "are saying about sin" is, on the whole, rather little, and that little mostly along lines that were well established just before or during the time of the Council. Recent Roman Catholic writings on the subject have been mostly popularizations of theories advocated around that time, or minor criticisms or modifications of them. Those theories themselves were, moreover, more or less conscious borrowings, with appropriate modification, from the far more radical speculations of liberal Protestant theologians since the Enlightenment. In great measure, typically modern Catholic thinking about sin has been not so much new as newly adopted and newly adapted. For Catholic theologians, the task of adaptation is that of relating modern speculations about sin, in some constructive way, to a long tradition of systematic and in certain respects dogmatic ecclesiastical teaching. It is an especially problematic tradition, with an especially complicated history. A drastically simplified summary of some of its main tenets may be the most practical way to introduce a book of this kind, intended for persons interested in theology but not professionally immersed in it. The purpose of the next few paragraphs is accordingly to recall major themes, categories, and issues that modern Catholic writers are likely to have in mind when approaching the subject of sin.

The prevalent notion of sin among Christians generally marks an area of convergence between religion and morality, two areas of thought which, we should remember, have not always seemed as distinct as they are considered to be in modern academic culture. Roughly speaking, sin has been thought of as human (or creaturely—to accommodate belief in sinful angels) wrongness, under the aspect of its offensiveness to God. Thus a sinner is a creature whose behavior or dispositions are in some measure disapproved or rejected by the Creator. Sinfulness can thus be regarded either as the object of God's disapprobation, or as the subject of estrangement from God. Insofar as God is thought of as revealing what he approves or wills, sin is conceived as non-conformity or disobedience to God. Thus the basic presuppositions of sin as usually understood are knowledge of the divine will or plan, together with sufficient freedom to abide by it or not. It is an easy step from this conception to envisaging the context of sin in legal or juridical terms, representing God as a supreme legislator and judge, and the sinner as a disloyal or disobedient subject who accordingly is, and is judged to be, guilty. This analogy, with its corresponding notions of God as law-maker and the sinner as law-breaker, is greatly developed in and under the influence of the Bible, against the background of a religion considered to have been founded on a covenant between God and his people. It has, as a result, greatly determined the dominant perspectives and typical idiom of Jewish, Christian, and Moslem deliberations about sin.

Early in the history of Christian thought, a distinction was made between the particular sins or sinfulness of individuals or groups and an underlying universal condition of sinfulness in which all (or nearly all—exceptions having been made for Jesus and Mary) persons participate. Although this distinction is not prominent in the Bible (or in characteristic teachings of Judaism), Christianity has regarded it as a crucial element of biblical revelation. Thus, mainly from certain passages in Paul's Letter to the Romans, and certain passages of Genesis to which they make allusion, early Christian theologians derived the idea of what came to be called original sin, meaning an inherent state of sinfulness that has beset all of humanity since, and because of, the "fall." The latter term refers to a definitive lapse from divine favor, incurred by the first human beings because of their disobedience to God's explicit orders. Thus, at the dawn of human history, Adam and Eve sinned, and a resultant sinfulness was transmitted to their descendants. The questions of what their sin was, how it gets transmitted, and in what form it is received have been the source of many theories, much controversy, and some dogmatic pronouncements.

Original sin, as just described, is traditionally contrasted with actual sin, which is the kind of sin referred to frequently in the Bible, comprising concrete, historical instances of human persons or groups of persons offending or disobeying God. Thus even original sin may be said to have started out as an actual sin, committed by Adam and Eve, but which, because of their position of ultimate human ancestry, had the peculiar property of devolving, as original sin, upon their descendants. Moreover, among subsequent human beings, original sin not only exists as the continuance of God's disfavor, but also entails a disordered religious and moral condition which facilitates, almost to the point of necessitating, frequent commission of actual sin. Thus it is sometimes remarked that in Christian theology not only are human beings sinners because they sin, but they also sin because they are sinners—where "sinners" refers in the former clause to actual sin and in the latter one to original sin.

Apart from its connectedness with original sin, actual sin has not been the subject of a great deal of fundamental theological speculation. Regarded as a violation of the divine will or an infraction of divine law, actual sin has been treated for the most part after the manner of normative ethics, but always with the understanding that the relevant norms are expressions, natural or supernatural, of the divine will. Once actual sin is understood, at least for practical purposes, as a kind of religious counterpart of illegality, it is inevitable that attention should be given to categorizing sins more or less as crimes are classified, and to distinguish degrees of seriousness, both according to different classes of offenses and according to different subjective conditions and circumstances in which the offenses are committed. Out of such considerations has arisen the traditional Catholic distinction between mortal and venial sin. The gradual development of an elaborate taxonomy of sin is mainly attributable to the practice of sacramental confession, where it represents an attempt to establish sufficiently precise terms of a common moral vocabulary for the requisite dialogue between penitent and confessor. For the same purpose, along with standard categories of sin, there was worked out a basic set of considerations relevant to assessing the seriousness of individual cases of sin, such as psychological dispositions and external circumstances that aggravate or extenuate personal fault. By far the greatest part of what Catholics have known as "moral theology" has been devoted to working out and applying procedures to specify actual sins and estimate the guilt they involve in concrete circumstances.

The interest that Christian doctrine takes in sin does not, of course, represent a morbid fascination with human badness in the sight of God. Christianity's central affirmation is its Gospel, or "good news," proclaiming that triumph over sin has been accomplished by God through the mission of Christ the Savior. Christian talk about sin is therefore strictly subordinate, but at the same time strictly indispensable, to Christian talk about salvation. One cannot meaningfully proclaim a message of salvation without some preestablished understanding of the object of that salvation. Salvation can be good news only for those who acknowledge a need for salvation. To put it even more crudely, salvation is propounded as the divine supply for a human demand; as Jesus himself put it, "those who are well have no need of a physician." Christianity's theology of sin is therefore an elaboration of its conviction that humanity as a whole is not well and has urgent need of a physician.

Accordingly, in Christian thought sin is constantly related to its remedy in Christ. As a message of reconciliation with God the Gospel must presuppose or preestablish a conviction of estrangement from God. As a declaration of forgiveness it must be predicated on an admission of guilt. Moreover, since in Roman Catholic theology the application of God's saving power to the individual sinner is understood to be mediated by personal faith, but also by those ritual "means of grace" that the Church identifies as sacraments, the understanding of human sinfulness must be expressed in terms appropriate to these ritual contexts. Consequently, Roman Catholic considerations of sin are, to a degree, shaped by Roman Catholic sacramental usage. This is an especially important factor with respect to the sacrament of penance, in which the ritual is constructed in the form of a dialogue between the penitent, who confesses sin, and the minister, who absolves from sin in virtue of divine empowerment. Evidently, the confession of sin required by this sacrament might, in theory, be expressed with varying degrees of generality and abstractness. However, it is Catholic teaching that for the integrity of the sacrament it is necessary for mortal sins to be confessed specifically and numerically. Consequently, the exigencies of the sacrament, thus understood, furnish highly practical motivation for moral theologians to devote themselves to the classificatory procedures referred to previously. Moreover, since Catholic theology represents the minister of the sacrament of penance as exercising a judicial (as well as a healing) function, sacramental practice tends to perpetuate an essentially juridical conception of sin. Not surprisingly, therefore, "what they are saying" about sin is in many respects closely involved with what they are saying about the sacrament of penance.

2
Sin and the Problem of Evil

What Christians are saying, and thinking, about sin is never altogether separable from what they say and think about evil in general.
Indeed, what has usually been meant by the problem of evil is most
intensely a problem for people who believe in the kind of God envis-
aged by biblical religion. For believers, sin constitutes from one point
of view part of the problem of evil. But from another point of view it
has often been thought of as part of the solution of the problem of evil.

Actually, the problem of evil can be conceived in two very different but equally basic senses. In the first sense, the phrase stands for a
practical problem, the problem presented to human beings everywhere
by their unavoidably frequent experiences of evil. This is simply the
problem which underlies all problems, of how to live as happily and
peacefully as all normal people wish to do, in a world that is thickly
strewn with occasions of suffering, frustration, and anxiety. In this
sense, the supreme instance of evil, and therefore the outstanding sym-
bol of it, has by most peoples been identified with death. And in this
sense the majority of religions, including Christianity, have offered
something purporting to be a solution to the practical problem of evil.
Thus, St. Paul's triumphant assertion that "death is swallowed up;
victory is won!" proclaims the Christian belief that death, here rep-

resenting the whole human experience of evil, and considered to be rooted in sin as its ultimate cause, has been effectively overcome and is on the way to being totally abolished by the redemptive intervention of God through Jesus Christ. For the Christian, therefore, who wholeheartedly believes this proclamation, evil is deprived of its characteristic force. Although evil remains for the Christian a part of life's experience, it becomes tolerable, and even in a sense negligible, in much the same way as the pangs of a disease from which the patient is fully convinced that he is on the way to permanent recovery. In this sense of the problem of evil, therefore, the Christian finds its solution in faith, and the subjective adequacy of the solution depends, for each individual, on the firmness and fullness of faith.

There is, however, another and more usual sense in which the problem of evil is rather a theoretical than a practical problem, and in this sense a number of religions, including Christianity, are especially affected by it. Although faith may, in the long run, provide a solution to the problem even in this sense, the problem can also be seen as posing a threat to faith itself. Insofar as it does threaten faith, it does so by suggesting that the claims of faith are ultimately irreconcilable with the demands of reason: that the implications of faith, confronted with the realities of experience, simply do not make sense.

The basic ingredients of the problem of evil in this latter sense are three assertions: first, that God is all-powerful; second, that God is all-good; and third, that evil does in fact surround us. A basic statement of the problem is to say that if any two of these three assertions are true, then the third one has to be false. Since a God who is all-good certainly could not want evil to exist, and a God who is all-powerful could certainly prevent evil from existing, the fact that evil does exist implies that God, if he also exists, must be limited in either his goodness or his power, and that the Christian notion of God must therefore be grossly mistaken.

It would be presumptuous to claim that Christian theology or philosophy has simply solved this problem, and most Christian thinkers would readily admit that the best reflection of the matter still

leaves a considerable area of mystery. Nevertheless, Christian efforts
to cope with the problem intellectually have established a number of
points of widely shared agreement.

Of the three assertions mentioned above, the one that Christian
theology has clung to most tenaciously and been least willing to qual-
ify is the assertion that God is perfectly good. The Christian Church
has invariably condemned theories which seek to modify this position
by allowing either that there is some kind of badness within God himself, or that, along with one or more good gods, there also exist, in a
kind of eternal competition, one or more bad gods.

Another logical possibility is, of course, to deny the reality of evil
itself. And although Christianity has never favored the idea that what
we identify as experiences of evil are simply illusions or misinterpre-
tations, a major tradition in Christian thought has insisted that evil
cannot be properly understood as a positive reality. The classic for-
mula of this tradition maintains that what we experience as evil is not
the presence of something intrinsically bad, but rather the absence of
some needed or wanted good. Evil has thus been philosophically
defined as a "deprivation of good"—the absence of something which,
in a plausible and intelligible sense, "ought" to be present. Although
this line of thought calls attention to a very important aspect of what
we mean by evil, and although by doing so it eliminates the implication that the existence of evil means that God produces it as a concrete
reality, nevertheless it cannot be said simply to solve the problem of
evil. For even if evil is best described as the "deprivation of good," the
question may still be reasonably asked why an all-good and all-powerful God does not prevent such deprivations from occurring. If one
claims, for example, that blindness, considered to be a physical evil, is
not an actual entity but simply the deprivation of sight, one may still
ask why a God who is limitless in power and goodness cannot or will
not prevent the creatures he normally endows with sight from suffering the loss or the lack of it.

One of the commoner ways of answering this sort of question has
been to point out that, as a matter of fact, physical evils often seem to

be indispensable for bringing about goods of a much higher order than those of which they are the deprivations. No doubt, many a blind person has been stimulated by his very affliction to be a much better person, on the whole, than he would otherwise have been. In more general terms, it seems hard to deny that without suffering some degree of evil, one's prospects for character development are rather poor. Traits like courage and patience constitute a great part of what is universally admired in human beings, and without the threat or presence of evil such traits could scarcely exist. It has been suggested, therefore, that God could indeed exclude all physical evil, but only if he were willing to settle for a completely unheroic humanity, a universe, so to speak, of "spoiled children." And, indeed, the very phrase "spoiled children" testifies to a common recognition that a certain amount of "deprivation of good" is, under ordinary circumstances, decidedly good for people. Given human beings as they generally are, it would be hard to deny that some experience of evil is virtually necessary to bring out the best in them, and not only their moral best, but the fullest development and exercise of their abilities generally. From this point of view the "hard knocks" of life have been often likened to a kind of natural training school. And for Christians, such training can readily be construed as a deliberate provision of divine providence. To apply this idea to the problem of evil, one might say that although God's power is sufficient to exclude every vestige of physical evil, he is deterred from doing so by his very goodness, in view of the fact that the resultant situation would not really be good for human creatures. Or, in other words, God is powerful enough to "spoil" his children, but he is too deeply good to do so.

Here again, however, we seem to have a kind of explanation that contains highly relevant and important insights, but that does not by any means completely solve the problem of evil. For, even though the experience of evil seems to bring out the best in some persons, in others it seems to bring out the worst. Moreover, if the experience of evil is thought of as experiencing a kind of divine training program, one is compelled to wonder why the rigors of training seem to be adminis-

tered so erratically and even unfairly. For whereas some of the train-
ees get off extremely lightly, for others severity is carried to the point
of overwhelming affliction. If the "school of hard knocks" appears to
toughen some of its pupils, it seems to crush a good many others, and
the distribution of toil and punishment is without apparent rhyme or
reason.

One approach to this problem that has often been adopted by
religious people is simply to maintain, by a kind of blind faith, that
since God must be just, everyone must, despite appearances to the
contrary, be getting precisely what he or she deserves. This approach
tends to emphasize, on the one hand, the deceptiveness of human
appearances generally and, on the other, the fact that God cannot be
fooled. God, who wants what is best for his human creatures, is the
only one who knows what is best for them. And since the physical
events of the universe are all in God's control, we must presume, even
when we cannot perceive, that everything happens for the best. From
this point of view, the difficulties of reconciling the facts of evil with
God's infinite power and goodness may seem to be mitigated, if not
actually eliminated, by invoking God's infinite wisdom and knowledge.
Thus, our perplexity at the distribution of suffering has been likened
to the perplexity of a small child being treated kindly and competently
by a physician who knows, as the child does not and cannot know, that
the only effective treatment is one that does entail pain. Accordingly,
we may say to ourselves about God what we might say to the child
about the physician—that he "knows best" what is good for us, and
does what is best for us regardless of our own misunderstandings.

A difficulty with this idea that our sufferings are part of God's
wise, kind, and powerful treatment is that such an idea seems to make
sense only if we presume that there is something so wrong with us in
the first place that such severe treatment is warranted by our condition. Thus, if God inflicts suffering on us as a good doctor inflicts suffering on his patient, we must have been ailing in the first place, and
ailing in a way for which such therapy is beneficial. But in that case,
it may seem, the problem of evil has only been pushed back, and not

solved, by saying in effect that God hurts us in order to cure us. For it seems not unreasonable to retort that an all-good and all-powerful God might have made us and kept us healthy enough to be spared his painful therapies. An omnipotent and benevolent physician might be expected to practice preventive medicine so perfectly as to make curative medicine unnecessary. And indeed, even the notion of suffering as a contribution to character formation seems to imply that the characters we start with in life must be rather ill-fashioned if only such rough use can prevent them from deteriorating or failing to develop. If, to do what is best for us, God must deal with us as harshly as he seems to do, it must be that we get off to a very bad start in life. And why should a God of boundless power and goodness get us started so badly? Granted that God should not content himself with spoiled children, might he not have provided himself with unspoilable children? If divine providence involves so much repair work and so many reform measures, are we not driven to conclude that divine creation must have been a somewhat botched-up job in the first place?

It is to this formulation of the problem of evil that Christian theological tradition has responded most typically. Basic to the traditional response is the idea that if God did not, in fact, produce a flawlessly perfect human machine by his act of creation, this is not because he is too unkind or too incompetent to do so, but because he intends to make something very much better than a perfect human machine, namely a human person. But the thing that chiefly distinguishes a person from a machine is the very thing that cannot be reconciled with God's creating "unspoilable children," namely freedom. For what has, in general, been traditionally meant by a person is a rational being who in some sense charts his own course and makes his own way through life. What a person is he becomes; what he becomes depends on what he does; and what he does depends on how he chooses. But this freedom which is a person's chief dignity is also his chief peril. For one who is free to choose is free to choose wrongly. One who chooses wrongly will act wrongly. And one who acts wrongly will produce bad effects. And since human persons are not only free beings but social beings, interacting within a shared environment, the bad effects of wrong actions and wrong choices on the part of individuals become part of the common environment and are shared by its occupants. They deprive that environment of some of the goodness it would otherwise enjoy, or, in other words, they introduce elements of evil which may, depending on circumstances, have very widespread consequences. And, as with the more prosaic kinds of environmental pollution, those who suffer most from the consequences may be among those who are least responsible for having produced them.

This way of approaching the problem of evil brings it within the perspective of a theology of sin. Traditionally, it has been closely related to the Christian doctrine of the fall, inspired by the early chapters of Genesis. However one interprets the details of that story, its theology is clearly concerned to affirm that God's creative work, sheerly good in itself, includes the creation of a being, called human, whose very excellence includes the power to disobey God and thereby distort his whole relationship with his origin, his destiny, and the fellow creatures who share his origin and destiny. The later doctrine of original sin, inspired mainly by St. Paul's Letter to the Romans, further implies that the consequences of human abuse of freedom are in some sense self-perpetuating, and irreparable by merely human efforts.

As applied to the problem of evil, these doctrines suggest that the relationship between the existence of evil and the power and goodness of God is a profoundly ironic one, inasmuch as personal freedom, the greatest natural benefit that God's power and goodness can confer, is inseparable from a potential abuse which is the root cause of evil. For Christianity as such, of course, theoretical insights into the problem of evil are always incidental and subordinate to the practical message of the Gospel: that the evil generated by the disobedient freedom of humanity finds its ultimate remedy in the obedient freedom of Jesus Christ, whose submission to the evil human beings inflict ultimately overcomes the evil human beings suffer.

3
Sin in Biblical Vocabulary

Like so many other theological concepts, the notion of sin has
been greatly influenced in modern Christian thought by intensified
interest and improved skill in interpreting the literature of the Bible.
In the past, Catholic theologians particularly tended to assume that
biblical writers must have thought about sin just as they themselves
had been taught to think about it. Such easy assumptions were based
in part on a naive confidence that dogmatic traditions faithfully transmitted biblical ideas even while clarifying and organizing them. They
were based also on very imperfect awareness of the literary complexity
of the Bible, as a work reflecting a wide variety of historical circumstances and expressing a considerable diversity of personal perspectives, in languages that continued to develop and that were at no point
simple equivalents of Western idioms. To review the biblical terms
that are or can be translated into English in terms of sin can be for
moral theologians an enlightening experience. It is quickly perceived
that there is no single Hebrew equivalent for the word "sin," that a
number of Hebrew words are translated by the single English word
"sin," and that these words were not originally religious expressions.
Rather their use in religious language was originally metaphorical.
Their distinctive overtones, reproducible only roughly if at all in translation, are best understood with reference to implicit comparisons.

15

Thus, for example, the most frequent Old Testament sin termi-nology (*ḥeṭ'* and its cognates) refers originally to "missing" or "fail-ing." It thus implies some directed action that does not achieve its proper aim or goal. It is employed literally, without religious or moral connotations, in describing the Benjaminite marksmen who "could sling a stone at a hair and not *miss*" (Jgs 20:16). Much more com-monly, however, it is part of the biblical language of morality. As such, it refers to failure in the discharge of a duty, or in the satisfac-tion of a legitimate claim, thus, roughly speaking, as the violation of a right. In this sense, the failure of duty constitutes an offense against the object of the duty, or the holder of the neglected claim or violated right. The offended claimant may be either another human being or God himself, as appears in the following passage where, in both clauses, the same verb is used: "If a man *sins against* a man, God will mediate for him; but if a man *sins against* the Lord, who can intercede for him?" (1 Sam 2:25). Thus the moral use of this terminology pre-supposes some norm governing some relationship. The "sin" therefore consists in an infraction of the norm, entailing a betrayal of the rela-tionship and an offense to the other party. In this sense, sin may even be quite unintentional, as when ignorance prevents the relationship from being correctly perceived and understood. A winsome example is the story of Balaam's failure to see the angel standing in his way, even though the ass he was riding did see it and objected verbally when his master tried to drive him on. Accordingly we are told that after "the Lord opened the eyes of Balaam" he confessed: "I have *sinned,* for I did not know that thou didst stand in the road" (Num 22:31, 34).

The second most frequent Old Testament language rendered in English terms of sin is more consistently metaphorical. Terms cognate with *'āwôn* are therefore not used in strictly juridical contexts, although they are frequently used theologically. Their literal reference is to crookedness, and their usage is similar to the employment of that term in English, as perjoratively contrasted with straightness or uprightness. This terminology is therefore used to indicate a defect not simply of behavior but of character, conceived as a perversion or distortion, and in this sense as an inner deformity, painful and shameful to bear, and translatable accordingly in terms of guilt, pressing or weighing one down. "For my *iniquities* ... weigh like a burden too heavy for me" (Ps 38:4). Conceived in this way as a burden, sin is easily thought of as being transferable, capable of being imposed on or assumed by another. Thus the scapegoat employed in a community ritual of atonement is said to "bear all their *iniquities* upon him to a solitary land" (Lev 16:22). In a similar fashion it is said of the Suffering Servant, in a passage which greatly influenced Christian theology, that "he bore the *sin* of many" (Is 53:12).

The third most frequent sin terminology in the Old Testament, like the first mentioned, presupposes a relationship secured by obligations. However, words related to *pāśa* direct attention more precisely to the relationship itself, for they refer to rupturing or breaking, as of contractual bonds. They therefore lend themselves to contexts of political rebellion, thought of as treaty violations, as when "Edon *revolted* from the rule of Judah" (2 Kgs 8:20, 22). In theological applications, this identification of sin as a breach of contract is particularly applicable to the fundamental Hebrew notion of God's relationship with his people as being formed and secured by a covenant.

Thus we have three favorite groups of terms pertaining to sin that focus respectively on the offense one person's sin inflicts on another, on the intrinsic damage sin does to the sinner, and on sin's destructive influence on relationships to whose demands it is a failure to conform. Quite a number of other Hebrew terms point metaphorically in similar and related directions. A term which means literally twisted recalls the familiar concept of distortion. Both the ideas of missing and of crookedness may be conceived more externally, as a disorientation of development or progress, a going off course, and thus expressed in terms of that straying which is so often associated with the misbehavior of sheep. Several other terms express the idea of sin as an act of dissidence or revolt. The notion of guilt may be referred to in language whose meaning is less psychological and more juridical, denoting the condition of one who comes under sentence of condemnation. The offensiveness of sin facilitates its being referred to as an abomination. Its contrast with rightness or normative truth associates it generically with the lie. And broader terms meaning evil and trouble are likewise applied with obvious appropriateness. In the wisdom literature, a distinctive vocabulary and point of view cause the term we translate as "folly" to possess a moral force the English equivalent largely obscures, and to overlap extensively with the domain of sin. We are reminded of the translational imparity by the perplexity most readers experience at Jesus' resounding condemnation of one who calls his brother a fool.

It would, no doubt, be quite wrong to suppose that the different connotations of these words are often clearly present to the minds of biblical writers, any more than users of English regularly distinguish among the dozens of rough equivalents to sin listed in *Roget's Thesaurus*. Series of them often appear in passages that represent no more than Hebrew taste for synonymous parallelism as a style of emphasis. Nonetheless, some sense of their etymological diversity contributes to an appreciation of the richness and subtlety of thought out of which this biblical vocabulary develops. And such appreciation should deter us from indiscriminately imposing and over-simplifying definitions.

For the sake of relative completeness, it should be noted that there is another and more mysterious category of biblical thought and language which may not strictly belong within the domain of sin, but which is closely related to and not always readily distinguishable from it. This is the category of uncleanness, frequently alluded to in ritual contexts, and applied to such things as corpses, sexual functions, skin diseases, and certain foods. Involvement with uncleanness has in common with sin the notion of overstepping certain bounds, with consequences that must be got rid of in order to resume a normal or socially acceptable condition. The roots of these ideas appear to be inaccessibly primitive and may be originally quite diverse. Association of the ideas of uncleanness and of sin is strengthened by the fact that washing is employed, figuratively and ritually, in connection with the removal of them both. A more basic relationship, therein implied, is suggested by the recognition of uncleanness as displeasing to God. Within the Bible, the sharpest difference between the two realms of thought is that instances of uncleanness cannot, while instances of sin can be interpreted in moral terms. This difference should not be obscured by the fact that both come within the scope of the law, which would only much later be conceived as having separate departments of ceremonial and ethical prescriptions.

In the New Testament, most references to sin use expressions related to the Greek word *hamartia*. Like the most frequent of the Old Testament words for sin, this terminology originally pertained to a physical "missing," in the sense of failing to reach an intended goal. The New Testament applies this language not only to acts that are misdirected, resulting in guilt and offense to God, but also to an underlying condition of enmity to God. It is perhaps by an intensification of this latter notion that sin is also represented as an active force abroad in the world, and personified in a number of figures of speech as something that attacks, occupies, or enslaves human beings.

There is a striking difference between the use of this language in the New Testament and in classical Greek literature. In the latter it is not so much a matter of moral irresponsibility, as of the human fallibility which makes possible, if not inevitable, all sorts of blunders, from the consequences of which life derives its tragedy, but by which it also imparts its lessons.

It has been suggested, particularly under the influence of the phenomenology of evil developed by Paul Ricoeur, that the human experiences reflected in the biblical vocabulary of sin can be usefully investigated and effectively related under three fundamental aspects—of defilement, sin proper, and guilt. The most primitive of these aspects, that of defilement, corresponds to a sense of having contracted a kind of stigma, not by any subjective ethical failing, but by a sort of contagion from without, such as is presupposed by the Hebrew regulations concerning uncleanness. The sense of being thus defiled is typically accompanied by a feeling of dread, implying expectation of imminent retribution. Given this state of mind, subsequent suffering is readily interpreted as an experience of vengeance or wrath unleashed by the circumstances of defilement. The problem of defilement calls for a solution, and this is typically provided by ritual procedures of purification.

The experience of sin, as distinct from but not unrelated to the experience of defilement, supposes the existence not merely of some powerful divine reality, but of a God whose relationship to human beings is one of personal encounter. In biblical literature, this presupposition is confirmed by the concept of the covenant, which involves not simply a belief in God, but an understanding of God as one who concerns himself with human beings and assumes the initiative in a divine-human dialogue. This understanding of God as one who encounters humanity in dialogue implies that God addresses human beings, and that they hear his words and respond. Responding to God's words is naturally conceived as heeding God's bidding, and the relationship between divine bidding and human heeding finds appropriate expression through the symbolism of law and obedience. The Old Testament clearly displays a development of thought from a simpler recognition of dialogical encounter with God to a moral theology of submitting to the detailed requirements of divine law, which became highly complex under the influence of rabbinical interpretation. But in this very process of development, the original sense of a human encounter with God is easily displaced by a view of the law itself as practically ultimate. This contrast may be perceived in considering the difference between hearkening to the prophets as proclaimers of God's immediate will, and looking to the law as the record of God's permanent requirements. In the same way, sin comes to be regarded less as a failure to respond to God than as a failure to conform to the law. If carried to the extreme, the religious foundation of sin disappears in such a process, being replaced by the mere notion of transgressing a heteronomous moral code.

If sin is regarded as an objective reality of the human condition before God, the subjective realization of that condition is represented by guilt. Guilt, like the subjective sense of defilement, involves a fearful apprehension of dire consequences, of a retribution that sin evokes and to which the sinner is subject. But it further involves a recognition of personal responsibility for those consequences, as brought about by an abuse of freedom, causing a breach in the divine-human dialogue.

4
Sin and the Covenant

Perhaps the most influential factor in modern Catholic thinking about sin has been a powerful combination of new awareness of certain aspects of Old Testament religion and new interest in certain aspects of modern religious existentialism. These trends of thought have been especially welcomed and cultivated by religious educators, with the result that they have penetrated popular religious culture remarkably quickly and deeply.

Looking first to popular understanding of the Bible itself, it is evident that, particularly among Catholics, the Hebrew idea of the covenant has come to be appreciated to a degree without precedent in the past. Earlier general neglect of this concept is, in fact, already hard to remember or even imagine. But if one surveys Catholic religious literature from before the present century, one will be struck by the infrequency of even incidental references to this idea. The basic reasons for its neglect are, of course, the peculiar way that the Old Testament was almost invariably read by Roman Catholic theologians in the past, and the fact that by Roman Catholic non-theologians it was read hardly at all. Theological use of the Old Testament was largely determined by apologetic purposes, which approached it as a body of inspired literature containing rather obscure messianic allusions that found their elucidation and fulfillment ' : Jesus Christ. In this perspective, the Old Testament was seen mainly as anticipating and thereby confirming the New Testament, which was thereupon treated as having, for all practical purposes, replaced it. Only occasionally and selectively was the Old Testament read as an immediate object of religious interest and source of religious understanding. Most pious laypersons did not read it at all, after having acquired in early childhood some acquaintance with a Bible history largely confined to narrative material in the Book of Genesis. Its place in the liturgy was narrowly restricted, and the material used was highly unrepresentative. Its direct influence on popular piety was mainly through fragmentary quotations and conventional, largely figurative interpretations.

All of this changed to a really astonishing degree less than a full generation ago, as a result of what is rather euphemistically referred to as the Catholic revival of biblical studies, actually the belated entry by Catholics into a biblical scholarship and biblical piety that had been thriving for some time under Protestant auspices. Catholic scholarship in this field was quickly perceived as furnishing rich pastoral resources, and, in collaboration with liturgical and catechetical reformers, it generated a vigorous new dimension of Catholic religious culture. In the interest of popularization, great attention was given to identifying and clarifying major themes of the biblical literature. Although in present retrospect this effort can be seen to have fostered some regrettable over-simplifications, it did make widely accessible an appreciation of those deeper currents of Old Testament religious thought which the New Testament rather presupposes than replaces.

In particular, the Hebrew religious conception of covenant became meaningful to Christians as it had seldom if ever been in the past. The law, especially as represented by the Decalogue, was perceived as something more than a detached set of divine moral prescriptions, being seen rather as a set of directions for preserving and improving a set of fundamental relationships that the covenant brought into being.

There can be little doubt that the new popular appreciation of covenant theology is especially indebted to biblical research and theory which interpret Old Testament usage in the light of certain ancient Near Eastern documents that illustrate the form of what are called suzerainty treaties. This terminology distinguishes them from examples of another and much more familiar type called the parity treaty. Parity treaties correspond to the familiar notion of a contractual arrangement between parties who deal with one another as equals. They are exemplified in political dealing between independent sovereignties who make certain prudent concessions to one another for what they suppose to be their mutual benefit. As long as that kind of arrangement represents what one means by a covenant, it is difficult to see how that term could have acquired the religious meaning it appears to have in the Old Testament. The God of the Hebrews is certainly not thought of as having approached his people to make, as it were, a fair deal between them and him. Between Yahweh and Israel there is infinite inequality. No contractual arrangement with his people could possibly benefit him. And the relationship between the people and their Lord is certainly not thought of as having been worked out through their mutual agreement.

What the suzerainty treaty represents as an analogy is a covenant between a great and powerful monarch and a relatively weak and vulnerable human community. What it establishes is a relationship of secure and stable dependence of those people upon that sovereign. It introduces a vassal status, predicated on a commitment to loyal allegiance as subjects. Characteristic formulations of such treaties introduce the suzerain by identifying titles of honor. They recall historical benefits that might inspire gratitude and trust. They stipulate that the new alliance must resolutely exclude all competitive allegiances. And they impose or endorse regulations designed to ensure the peaceful coherence of the community that is to assume the duties and prerogatives of vassal fidelity.

Whether or not historical documents of this kind did in fact furnish paradigms for the covenant conception in Hebrew religion, they do exemplify a pattern of thought that makes that conception consistently intelligible. The Hebrew covenant is conceived not as a reciprocal arrangement, but as an act of divine initiative and condescension. Its exalted author is "the Lord your God," whose unmerited intervention "brought you out of the land of Egypt, out of the house of bondage." It sternly abolishes all conflicting allegiances to alien lords: "You shall not have strange gods before me." And it imposes a set of rules, the laws that are evidently designed to preserve good order and sound relationships among the people who, in virtue of the covenant, become in a uniquely privileged sense "the people of God." The terms of the covenant are the indispensable prerequisites for enjoying that life, progress, and prosperity which the Lord promises to his faithful subjects.

Against such a background of thought, sin remains describable as the breaking of the law. But breaking the law implies much more than simply violating arbitrary regulations, imposed and sanctioned from on high. Breaking the law means breaking down the covenant and breaking up that whole system of vital relationships that is founded on the covenant. Sin becomes, in its most essential meaning, infidelity. And infidelity becomes, in virtue of what the covenant is understood to be, both supreme ingratitude and supreme folly, despising the greatest of benefactors and forfeiting the greatest of benefits. And since the covenant is the alliance of a people, those obligations which secure the people's social coherence are inseparable from the bonds that link them to their Lord. It is all of a piece, so that every betrayal of one's fellow subject is a betrayal of the Lord, and every betrayal of the Lord is a betrayal of one's fellow subject. Within the covenant, loyalty to God and loyalty to neighbor are inseparable. There is no legitimate distinction between anti-social behavior and irreligious behavior.

It is an easy transition from this kind of thinking to the New Testament's teaching of a twofold law of love, of God and of neighbor, whereby the whole law is comprised. Insofar as the covenant and the law are conceived along the lines just described, sin, as violation of the law, has to be perceived as a personal and social offense. Since the covenant is a gift of gracious love, and since the law is intrinsic to that gift, all sin, as an infraction of the law, expresses ingratitude, disloyalty, and faithlessness.

This conception of sin, as betraying a covenant of love, finds even more poignant expression in the metaphor, developed by the prophets, of the covenant as a marriage bond, whereby God joins his people to himself in permanent, loving union. Insofar as marriage is a figure of the covenant, sin takes on the infamous associations of conjugal infidelity. Violation of the covenant is thus likened to adultery, and a life of infidelity to a career of prostitution.

On this basis, the covenant relationship between God and his people is readily assimilated to what modern personalist existentialism, itself rooted in Jewish biblical piety, has accustomed us to call an "I-Thou" relationship. Within that perspective, sin may still indeed be referred to as a breaking of God's law, but that phrase no longer sustains impersonal, legalistic connotations.

By the same token, the confession, repentance, and forgiveness of a sinner is more readily appreciated as a kind of divine-human dialogue whereby a personal relationship, shattered by infidelity, is reestablished and resumed. A personalist conception of sin is prerequisite to an authentically religious understanding of reconciliation. For reconciliation precisely means the restoration of friendship where there has been enmity, the resumption of intimacy where there has been alienation.

The contribution of these trends of thought to pastoral ministry is probably most evident in recent Catholic reorientation of what was traditionally called the sacrament of penance but recently renamed the sacrament of reconciliation. Emphasis on reconciliation, rightly understood, strongly discourages that unwholesome preoccupation with detailed self-incrimination which long characterized Catholic attitudes toward the sacrament that most people were accustomed to call neither penance nor reconciliation, but, significantly, confession. It likewise precludes the semi-magical interpretation of priestly absolution as a taking away of sins comparable to the erasure of censures from a discreditable record. Once it is conceived as a dialogue of reconciliation, the sacrament becomes comprehensible as an occasion of prayer, and only on that basis can it be comprehensible as liturgy.

There is another respect also, in which the conception of sin as violation of the covenant lends itself to a richer interpretation of liturgical repentance. For, given that understanding of the covenant which has just been reviewed, it is clear that one who acts disloyally toward the covenant offends not only God but the rest of the community as well. Consequently, reconciliation must likewise be with the community as well as with God. And that is significantly in harmony with a traditional understanding of the sacrament of reconciliation as intending the sinner's reunion, or improved union, both with God and with the Church.

In the history of Christianity, as in the history of Israel, there is a recurrent temptation to allow concern with the law to become detached from concern with that covenant from which the law derives its meaning and value. To the extent that this occurs, religious morality degenerates into a form of legalism. Sin becomes a matter of rule-breaking, and the assessment of sinfulness becomes, according to the temperament of the one who makes it, either sophistical or scrupulous. And in either case, attention to sin serves to deepen that very self-centeredness in which sin most flourishes. It makes a world of difference whether sin is primarily conceived as transgressing Something or as betraying Someone. And that difference penetrates to the very heart of religion itself.

The covenant, as used theologically, is, of course, a metaphor. And sin, thought of as covenant disloyalty, is a metaphor within a metaphor. To deal with these terms literally would be misleading and, carried beyond a certain point, plainly absurd. But it can be even more misleading to suppose that such metaphorical language about sin can be somehow translated or transposed into expressions that are not figurative at all. As long as we try to make any statements about a God who we believe utterly transcends our experience, or about any-

thing else precisely in its relationship to God, we are compelled to settle for figures of speech, metaphors, analogies. The important thing is
not to abolish the metaphors, but to cultivate those that do fullest justice to our religious experience and our faith. That there may be more
adequate ways to talk about sin than in terms of a covenant is entirely
possible. But that there are less adequate ways, and that they have
often been used, is entirely clear.

5
Temptation and Concupiscence

In the past, when Christians talked about sin in practical terms, and especially when they preached about it, frequent reference was made to what is called "temptation." Basically, temptation was thought of as the motivation for sin. Although sinning was regarded as an abuse of human freedom, the decision to sin is evidently not an exercise of sheerly arbitrary malice. Sinners have their reasons for sinning, and those reasons are to be found in circumstances which constitute an inducement to sin, offering some kind of advantage to sinful conduct. But the word "temptation," in religious usage, implies more than simply a stimulus to sinful behavior. It implies a theological interpretation of such stimuli, and that interpretation has had a complex history.

The whole range of ideas associated with temptation is largely anticipated in the Bible. Although the relevant Hebrew terms of the Old Testament have their verbal equivalents in Greek vocabulary, the biblical usage goes far beyond that of secular Greek. In English, the word "tempt" is closely related to the word "attempt," and the basic idea of temptation is, in the most general sense, the idea of trying. That idea leads naturally to the more complex notion of discerning or demonstrating something by means of trial, or, in the simplest sense of the word, experiment.

The main features of the original idea are well-exhibited by the familiar biblical metaphor taken from metallurgy. It refers to a technique whereby a sample of metal or metallic ore was tested by means of fire. The procedure was carried out by an artisan for the twofold purpose of assaying and refining, that is, of analyzing the contents and getting rid of those which are considered impurities. Thus the whole process is at once a method of proof and a method of improvement. It is this familiar practice that is referred to by the Lord's words to Jeremiah, "I will refine them and test them," and in Isaiah's prophecy, "I have refined you, but not like silver; I have tried you in the furnace of affliction." As combining the ideas of assaying and refining, this metaphor serves a purpose similar to that of other biblical figures of speech applied to divine judgment, expressed as the separation of a mixture into its desirable and its undesirable components, such as the grain and the chaff, the wheat and the tares, the sheep and the goats, the barren and the fruitful trees.

The earliest theological uses of the temptation motif in the Bible are related to covenant theology. Repeatedly, the sufferings of the exodus are interpreted as testings or temptings. God does the testing; his people undergo it. They are tested by sufferings and threats of suffering, from natural and human dangers. What is being tested is the covenant virtue, fidelity, or faith, their passive reliance on God's providence and active obedience to his commands. Ironically, the people's most decisive failure of that test is expressed in terms of their "tempting" God. The motif of tempting and testing is read back into the narratives of the patriarchs, most dramatically in the case of Abraham's being summoned to sacrifice his son Isaac. It is clearly an important aspect of the Garden of Eden story, although the language of temptation is not explicitly used of the test that Eve and Adam underwent and failed. In the later apocalyptic literature, temptation operates within an eschatological context and is surrounded with mythological elements, but it remains an ordeal that tests fidelity, offering experimental evidence for divine judgment. In this literature, satanic or diabolic agencies of temptation are often conspicuous.

But it was, of course, a quite different kind of Satan who first entered the biblical literature in the story of Job, the whole dramatic structure of which is determined by the motif of temptation. Satan is seen in the prologue as the one who conceives and executes the whole design of Job's temptation, but who does so as God's functionary, entirely subject to God's authorization. What this prologue seems to express is the author's reluctance to present God straightforwardly as Job's tempter, tester, and tormentor. In this and other Old Testament uses of Satan as tempter, we may see a mythological effort to ease a tension in the writers' minds between their understanding of temptation and their understanding of God. Since God's sovereignty must be maintained, what happens to Job must happen by God's will. But the rather shocking implications are softened and obscured by representing Satan as the deviser and executor of the scheme which God reluctantly approves. In the poetic dialogue that constitutes most of the Book of Job, no such inhibitions are operative, and Satan's role is not even referred to. Similar uses of Satan to extenuate, as it were, God's complicity in temptation occur elsewhere in the Old Testament. But in the last analysis, if Satan is under God's control, satanic temptations must be divine temptations, and introducing Satan as an intermediary between God and the victims of temptation can be only diversionary rhetoric, and no real explanation of how, or why, God makes himself responsible for the ordeals of temptation. Indeed, if God is what the Bible conceives God to be, it is unintelligible that temptation could provide him with information that he would otherwise lack; clearly omniscience makes experimentation unnecessary.

It is probably some such line of thought that has led to increasing abandonment of the language of temptation in theological discussions of sin. Nevertheless, there are adaptations of the idea of temptation that are not vulnerable to such criticism, and which do appear in the Bible. Especially in the wisdom literature we find a different basis for regarding temptation as part of the divine plan and as designed to furnish a kind of experimental knowledge. But it is thought of as furnishing knowledge not to God, who does not need it, but to human

beings, who do. Thus God provides temptation to implement his function not as our judge, but as our teacher. It is we, rather than God,
who learn from our own responses to the circumstances that test and
try us. The connection between undergoing distressing ordeals and
deepening self-knowledge is one that most people are ready to concede. And that connection is closely related to another, also widely
appreciated, between the successful undergoing of painful ordeals and
the development of virtue. Thus, in the perspective of some of the wisdom writings, temptation is an ingredient of life which, however
uncomfortable, is indispensable for moral growth. The circumstances
we call temptations constitute a natural demand and stimulus for that
measure of asceticism without which there can be neither depth of
self-knowledge nor firmness of self-control.

Understood in this way, temptations become at once lessons and
tests in the school of life. What they test is obedience to the known
will of God. And it is in passing such tests that obedience is strengthened to meet future tests. They are thus fitted into a divine plan that
is seen as a kind of training program for the development of what God
intends human beings to become. The difficulty that tends to arise for
this interpretation is not theoretical but practical. It is the average
human being's notoriously poor record in profiting by this training
program and in passing its tests. Temptations are obviously suc-
cumbed to, rather often, even by persons of the greatest moral and
religious earnestness. Despite good will and hard effort, human beings
manifest a chronic weakness in the face of temptation, amounting to
a very limited ability to do, habitually, what they are themselves convinced they ought to do. In moments of candor, most people can readily make their own St. Paul's confession, "I do not do what I want,
but I do the very thing I hate." And St. Paul's reflection that somehow
inside himself there appeared to be "another law at war with the law
of my mind" recalls a common phrase of those who give way to temptation, "I don't know what got into me!"

Thus, consideration of temptation has led to the idea that there
is something wrong, generally and intrinsically, with human beings as

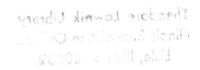

we know them that makes it very easy for them to go wrong even when they know better and try hard. Jewish writers have long referred to this factor, with a phrase taken from the Bible, as an "evil inclination" or "evil imagination" that is operative within us all. This perverse inner tendency, whose strength is evidenced primarily by the weakness of our resistance to temptation, became a traditional Jewish explanation of the frequency of sin. Its equivalent in Christian theological usage is the term "concupiscence," conceived as a powerful inner drive or appetite that urges us toward its gratification, even when its gratification can be secured only by forbidden means.

New Testament references to "concupiscence" are translations of the Greek term *epithumia,* which broadly corresponds to the Hebrew *yēzer hā-ra,* signifying what was previously referred to as the "evil inclination." Nevertheless, in Jewish thought it was not universally supposed that the *yēzer,* as an ingredient of human life, must be altogether a bad thing. And although some Jewish writers went so far as to equate this inner drive with Satan himself, it appeared to others that the powerful appetite which in certain circumstances resisted God's law was not intrinsically different from that general drive toward satisfaction which can also motivate perfectly innocent human strivings. Thus, in Jewish usage, a distinction was made between good and bad *yēzer,* or, more precisely, between the good and bad, the permitted and forbidden tendencies of a drive or appetite that, considered in itself, is morally and religiously neutral. Conceived in this way, one would seem to be describing an aspect of human psychology very like what in Freudian usage is called *libido,* an essentially undifferentiated reserve of psychic energy which can be directed in morally opposite ways.

Although some early Christian writers use the term "concupiscence" in a similar morally neutral sense, the corresponding term in the New Testament always has a morally negative force—not surprisingly, since it is always introduced in the context of temptation and sin. Christian theology has, for the most part, regarded concupiscence only as a moral and religious liability. And that usage became especially entrenched under the powerful influence of St. Augustine, who regarded concupiscence as a proneness to evil cravings that is part of the tragic legacy from the sin of our first parents. A curious result of this Augustinian theology is that whereas Jews looked to the *yēzer* for an explanation of how Adam could have transgressed God's command, Christians have looked to Adam's transgression for an explanation of why his descendants experience concupiscence! Each of these approaches can raise a problem. For the former approach, the problem is why Adam, before his transgression, should have had any *yēzer* to get him into trouble. For the latter approach, the problem is why, lacking concupiscence, Adam should ever have yielded to temptation. The former problem seems at least less acute if one thinks of the *yēzer* as morally neutral psychic energy, for without some kind of basic, general drive toward self-satisfaction, it is hard to see how there could have existed what we normally mean by human life at all. Indeed, some of the rabbis, noting that one important aspect of the *yēzer* is obviously the sex drive, have pointed out that its elimination would put an end not only to human lust, but also to human life! A facetious remark, perhaps, but one that makes an important point often neglected by Christian theologians in their remarks about concupiscence.

As a matter of fact, recent Roman Catholic theology, in investigating the significance of concupiscence in the Council of Trent's doctrine concerning original sin, has in some instances moved much closer to the Jewish conception of a drive or craving that is by no means evil in itself, but which may in certain circumstances gravitate toward or adhere to its object with a relentlessness that gravely inhibits morally right behavior. In this sense, concupiscence may be thought of as a kind of dynamic inertia in human craving, which may well facilitate good behavior as long as its object is innocent, but which, when its object is forbidden, may be overcome only by considerable moral exertion. It is cases of the latter kind that are referred to as temptations.

Understanding concupiscence as the force behind temptation is implied at a number of points in the New Testament. It is in the Letter of James that it is most explicitly a point of doctrine. That letter begins by telling its readers to rejoice when they meet "various trials." The trials are interpreted as testings of faith, which produce a "steadfastness" whose full effect is perfection. The use of a term like steadfastness to express the happy outcome of the trials suggests that they are thought of primarily as sufferings to be endured rather than as tasks to be performed. This teaching is reminiscent of the wisdom literature, and indeed it is immediately followed by the advice to ask God confidently for wisdom. The wisdom literature is clearly the inspiration of the beatitude pronounced a few verses later on "the man who endures trial" because "when he has stood the test he will receive the crown of life." But at this point, even though the writer has been giving a favorable account of trials, he warns that "no one may say when he is tempted, 'I am tempted by God'; for God cannot be tempted with evil and he himself tempts no one." The obvious question—If God does not tempt, then who does?—is then answered in a way that reminds us of the rabbinical speculations already referred to. "Each person is tempted when he is lured and enticed by his own desire." This desire is then put in a bad light, as something that, "when it has conceived, gives birth to sin; and sin, when it is full-grown, brings forth death." It is probably to explain why temptation, having its source in such malignant desire, cannot be from God, that the author then asserts that "every good endowment and every perfect gift is from above."

In this passage, the Bible's fullest statement on temptation and its relationship to concupiscence, we have, first of all, the idea of a testing of faith, so beneficial and salvific that it could certainly be included among God's gifts. But just afterward we have the idea of a tempting derived not from God, but from a human desire that leads to sin and death. Thus the passage, taken as a whole, answers questions about temptation in a way that raises other questions. There are trials that are salutary, to be rejoiced over, and therefore presumably God-sent. But there are also temptations, not God-sent, but arising from a personal desire that spawns sin and death. To the two most obvious questions, James gives no solution. First, how do the good, God-sent trials work, if not on the basis of human desire? And, second, where could the human desire that produces ungodly temptations come from, if not from God? Rabbinical writers, as we have seen, found a principle of compatibility for such different ideas in their conception of a morally neutral or ambivalent drive or appetite, created by God as part of human psychology, but having to be resisted insofar as its tendencies are irreconcilable with moral and religious duty. Some Christian theologians appear to be moving in the direction of a similar solution, somewhat complicated in their case by traditional usages associated with the doctrine of original sin.

6
Original Sin and Psychology of the Unconscious

Recent theological treatments of original sin have tended on the whole to present it less as an essentially mysterious datum of supernatural revelation and more as a phenomenon of common human experience. Accordingly, typically modern writers have given less attention to what is traditionally called *peccatum originale originans,* the starting point or originating moment of original sin, and more attention to *peccatum originale originatum,* the abiding condition of human life considered to have been thus originated. This condition is thought of as a state of religious and moral impairment, entailing a disrupted relationship with God and manifested in distressingly unavoidable discrepancies between spiritual aspiration and achievement. A recurrent theme in the world's literature records the often anguished failures of human beings to realize in practice their own ideals by conforming their behavior to norms of conduct whose validity they freely and fully accept. Perhaps the most frequently cited example is St. Paul's moving account in Romans, often, though arguably, assumed to be autobiographical, of discovering within oneself two radically incompatible imperatives, one pressing compellingly toward evil, and the other summoning ineffectually toward good.

37

Paul's account of this kind of experience brings out with remarkable vividness the sense of a divided self, within which unauthorized cravings seem to struggle with dismaying effectiveness against the practical determinations of rational and religious morality. These rebellious forces that appear to underlie so much of what is most deplored in human conduct have been collectively termed "concupiscence," in the sense of unruly appetite or undisciplined desire. It has been often remarked that this aspect of human experience is realized socially as well as individually, finding expression in the concerted behavior of human groups, and appearing to perpetuate or propagate itself from one generation to the next as a grim constant among the variables of human history.

It would seem natural that phenomena of this kind should attract the attention of social scientists and particularly of psychologists. Yet in the past, the science of psychology has shown little interest in, and shed little light on, the matter. Recently, however, psychology has been looked to much more hopefully for relevant observations and explanations. The newness of this interest finds its plainest explanation in the emergence during the past century of new schools of thought in psychology, formed around theories and techniques for exploring the unconscious as a hitherto neglected source of dynamic influences on human behavior.

Of these modern schools of thought in psychology, psychoanalysis, the earliest and most celebrated, attracted the attention of theologians and religious thinkers almost from the start. Much of that attention was and is hostile and suspicious, especially on account of Freud's anti-religious philosophy and what many judged to be his unwholesome preoccupation with sex. At the same time, there was a more positive and more thoughtful reaction on the part of a number of moral theologians, who perceived in Freud's account of unconscious motivation a largely overlooked factor whose limiting effect on human freedom could reduce or exclude the subjective culpability of objectively immoral actions. Similar considerations made pastoral counselors and confessors more wisely hesitant in assessing the moral condition of their clients. In these connections, what are now familiar insights of Freudian psychology have been applied mainly to practical dealings with what is called actual, as distinguished from original, sin. Such applications have not directly affected theological doctrine as such, being readily accommodated as new data within a preestablished framework of thought about the bearing of freedom, and therefore of any factors modifying freedom, on subjective sinfulness in concrete behavior. Consideration of such new data has undoubtedly influenced typically modern speculation about the practicality, as distinct from the theoretical validity, of distinguishing between mortal and venial sin, and about how, how easily, and how often truly mortal sins are likely to occur. Pressed in certain directions, this trend of thought fosters a certain diffidence, sometimes denounced as laxity, in both the pastoral denunciation of sin and the penitential acknowledgement of it. More specific attention to the state of these and related questions will be given elsewhere.

In addition, however, to the application of very general psychoanalytic perspectives to actual sin, increasing interest has been taken in clarifying the empirical aspect of original sin by relating it to psychoanalytic accounts of the structure and development of human personality. With special reference to Roman Catholic theology of original sin, this approach is exemplified with particular thoroughness and consistency by Sharon MacIsaac's book, *Freud and Original Sin.* MacIsaac adopts the Scholastic distinction between a formal and a material aspect of *peccatum originale originatum.* The formal aspect is understood to be the deprivation of a right relationship with God, and as such it cannot, of course, find a place within Freudian theory. But it is otherwise with the material aspect, identified with concupiscence, conflicting with the rational exercise of human freedom and thereby having a disruptive effect on both the inner integrity of personality and the social harmony of human relations. There is an unmistakable resemblance between representative descriptions of this condition and the kind of self-alienation that is dealt with, both theoretically and clinically, by psychoanalysis. Insofar as psychoanalysis is thought to illuminate these phenomena, it may be judged by Christians to render more intelligible the comparable features of original sin.

It is well known that psychoanalytic theory postulates three basic components of personality—id, ego, and superego. Of these the oldest is said to be the id, an unconscious, primitive reservoir of psychic energy which operates in accordance with the "pleasure principle," achieving a reduction of painful tension by the acquirement of immediate hedonic gratification. Out of this crude but fundamental dynamism there is said to evolve a strikingly different structure known as the ego, largely conscious and systematically organized, which operates in accordance with the "reality principle," a kind of basic prudence, ready to forego or postpone immediate gratifications and endure the resulting tension in the interest of achieving in the long run a broadly preferable state of affairs. The ego serves therefore as a corrective of the id, but since it also derives from it, it does not extinguish the pleasure principle, and the reality principle may often conflict with and succumb to it in practice.

The compatibility of this account with familiar descriptions of concupiscence in action is so obvious that it is impossible not to conjecture that the same kind of experience is being treated from a different viewpoint and in a different idiom. To the extent that this conjecture is accepted, one may find in the literature of psychoanalysis further and perhaps fuller or subtler descriptions of the lustings of the flesh against the spirit. But from a theological point of view what is more important is the stark contrast between the explanations of such phenomena given by psychoanalysis and by Christian tradition. In particular, the Freudian account finds no need to postulate any fall from a previously superior human condition. Indeed, the conflict between id and ego is seen rather as a positive developmental phenomenon than as a symptom of deterioration. In the last analysis, therefore, adoption of the Freudian perspective makes it unnecessary and inappropriate to think of concupiscence as originating from or as partly constituting anything we should normally think of describing as sin. This does not, of course, mean that concupiscence is deprived of all relationship to sin. But its obvious relationship would be antecedent rather than consequent, and to actual rather than original sin. The strivings of a reality principle against a pleasure principle are readily interpreted in terms of moral exertion based on ethical choice. But the necessity of such exertion and the difficulty of such choice would be seen as part of the normal and natural development of maturing human personalities, rather than as the legacy of a primordially wounded nature. The presupposition would not be that of a lost perfection, but that of an originally imperfect and strenuously improvable human condition. The fact that individuals evidently differ in the degree in which they suffer from this condition is in agreement with a traditional understanding that, although all human beings share in original sin equally, they experience concupiscence unequally on account of their constitutional and environmental diversity.

The doctrine of original sin is a way of answering, however mysteriously, a question not only about what is wrong with the moral and religious lives of human beings, but also about where that wrongness comes from. And under this aspect as well, it has been suggested that psychoanalysis offers instructive insights. Particularly relevant in this connection is Freud's strong insistence on the extreme susceptibility of early childhood to environmental influences, and in particular to certain types of influence characteristic of interaction between parents and children. Freud has greatly intensified popular conviction that parents transmit to their offspring, often quite unwittingly, many basic elements of the culture they are destined to share, and that they do so long before any rational communication with them becomes possible. And since the parents of one generation were the children of a preceding one, this process of transmission is a vital part not only of individual but of racial history. As children mature, the influence upon them of others, whether elders or peers, is increasingly mediated by understood language and by examples consciously reflected upon. But in early childhood, and always to some degree, much subtler social influences, not perceived as such, have profoundly formative effects.

There is, therefore, in addition to biologically genetic inheritance, a rich psychological legacy that is appropriated pre-critically, unconsciously, and involuntarily. Such a legacy has, of course, both peculiar elements corresponding to the individual differences of particular persons involved, and common features reflecting participation in a larger society. From both sources it derives weaknesses as well as strengths, ineptitudes as well as aptitudes, for the living of a fully satisfactory human life. Among the inherited liabilities are propensities toward what, rationally, morally, and religiously, are regarded as folly, vice, and sin.

Here again, such notions popularized by psychoanalysis have definite though only partial applicability to traditional Christian thinking about original sin. In Catholic theology, original sin is said to be transmitted by "propagation" as distinct from "imitation." Although the Catholic dogma of Mary's immaculate conception reminds us that the effect of this propagation is believed to occur at the very moment of biological conception, there is here again room for distinguishing between a formal and a material aspect. Since the former is not empirically observable, it can have no explicit role in the theories of social science, and since it is supposed to become a reality at the very inception of individual human existence, it cannot be thought of as a developmental feature. It is, however, quite otherwise with that material aspect of original sin, referred to the idea of concupiscence, which does belong to the realm of human psychological and social experience.

As already suggested, classic descriptions of concupiscence invite comparison with psychoanalytic descriptions of a self-alienation explained in terms of conflict between a preestablished id and a gradually emergent ego. This ego emerges in response to an environment that, in its beginnings, is powerfully dominated by parental influences which are themselves highly responsive to an antecedent culture. Among these influences, moreover, some take the form of a more or less deliberate discipline, inculcated by rewarding and punishing behavior that accompanies parental expressions of approval and disapproval. Insofar as this disciplinary influence is spontaneously interiorized, a third basic personality structure, the superego, takes its place with ego and id as a kind of internal censor, inhibiting those kinds of behavior that have been systematically opposed, and fostering those that have been treated with favor. This sort of primitive or pre-reflective conscience obviously opens the way to a further dimension of interior conflict in which both the pleasure principle and the reality principle may become embroiled. Moreover, since the originating influences represent not only the peculiar preferences of parents, but the social mores by which they participate in their culture, what is transmitted is a cultural as well as a personal legacy, and ensuing conflicts may have broadly social as well as intimately personal implications. Thus, the moral strengths and weaknesses, harmonies and discordances of society itself are seen to be, in a meaningful though not strictly biological sense, propagated. However autonomously one may finally choose among ethical options, there is an antecedent moral and social heritage that can be neither avoided nor totally transcended. As will appear in a later discussion, recent theological theorizing about a broadly social dimension of original sin, referred to as "sin of the world," has special relevance to this connection with psychoanalytic explanations. So too, does the recent emphasis on "sinful social structures" in writings by Christian ethicists and moral theologians, even though what they primarily envisage is actual rather than original sin.

Perhaps the most recurrent assertion of those who know almost but not quite nothing about Freudian psychoanalysis is to the effect that it reduces everything to sex. Although not very illuminating and potentially quite misleading, this is true, insofar as Freud identifies as sexual, in a very broad sense, the most basic energies of the psyche, as implied by his calling "libido" the instinctual dynamism of the id. Although pan-sexualism has been a rallying cry for many anti-Freudian Christians, it has not escaped notice that traditional Christian discussions of original sin, especially under St. Augustine's influence, have themselves paid an extraordinary amount of attention to sex. This has been due partly to certain interpretations of the Adam and Eve story, partly to the sexual modality of that "propagation" whereby original sin is said to be transmitted, and partly to the vivid way that strong sexual spontaneity illustrates the conception of concupiscence as a kind of carnal rebelliousness. In a sense, this common preoccupation of psychoanalysts and theologians of original sin may serve to encourage psychoanalytically oriented interpretations of original sin such as have just been discussed. But beyond this superficial similarity of outlook, it may be that Freud's discussions of the normal development of basically sexual energies from originally hedonistic to ultimately altruistic modes of expression furnishes a desired antidote to Christian theology's grim view of sex and rather grudging acceptance of even its most wholesome employments. Under this aspect, concupiscence itself may be perceived, despite its undoubted contributions to sin and vice, as containing the indispensable seed of that same love to which Christianity pays highest honor as the very antithesis of sin and vice. Thus, Christian advocates of Freudian reinterpretations of original sin are inclined to ask whether ecclesiastical disparagement of psychoanalysis for its emphasis on sex does not depend on an attitude toward sex that psychoanalysts do not typically share, and which an application of their theories to the doctrine of original sin might helpfully correct.

7
Original Sin and the World's Sin

Among the many oddities Catholics owe to the English translation of their Mass is an inconsistency between the Gloria, where Christ is said to take away "the sin of the world," and the Agnus Dei, where he is said to take away "the sins of the world." Only the most alert worshipers recite both correctly! The plural form, "sins," was accurately translated from the Latin text that preceded it. But the singular looks beyond the Latin to its own source in the Greek of the Fourth Gospel, where the Baptist is reported to have said at his first sight of Jesus, "Behold, the Lamb of God, who takes away the sin of the world!" As biblical interpreters have often pointed out, the plural would refer to sinful acts, whereas the singular refers to a sinful condition. It is in this sense, of a sinful condition, that "the sin of the world" is referred to by modern Catholic theologians who have firmly established it in the technical vocabulary of modern speculation concerning original sin. This speculation has already generated quite a variety of subtly different theories, and it is still in a very fluid state; nevertheless, certain trends of thought have been notably persistent, and we shall confine our discussion for the most part to them.

Despite our explicit doctrines about original sin's nature, origin, and transmission, few people have found the ideas and explanations

45

easy to relate to their familiar ways of thoughts and kinds of experience. Why and how the misbehavior of an ancestral couple should alienate all their descendants from God and leave them mentally and morally rather incompetent has probably perplexed every new generation of catechumens who allowed themselves to think about it. Traditional explanations to the effect that we were all somehow "in Adam's loins" in such a way that his sin gets passed along in the very process of procreation only seem to make matters worse. Innumerable discussions of the matter have ended with believers bowing their heads to what they concede to be mystery—and with unbelievers shaking their heads over what they conceive to be nonsense.

But at the same time, a great many people who find the doctrinal formulations completely unilluminating are quite ready to acknowledge that the idea of original sin draws attention to a very disconcerting aspect of reality. For it seems plain enough that, however it gets there, sin does manage to turn up everyplace. Neither self-knowledge, nor social experience, nor acquaintance with history provides much evidence of any sustained innocence in human character and behavior.

Both literary theories, as applied to biblical mythology, and biological theories, as applied to the origin of species, have weakened Christian belief in a literally first man and woman of whom all other human beings are the direct descendants. For this reason also, traditional accounts of original sin have been received with increasing incredulity. Some theologians have accordingly abandoned monogenism (the theory of ultimate derivation from a single human pair), while observing that, however our biological origins may be traced, there must at some point have arrived on the scene some creatures of our kind who, like us, discovered in themselves a freedom capable of resisting God's bidding, and who abused that freedom, presuming in their self-assertion to "be like God, knowing good and evil." In other words, sin, since it is obviously with us now, must have got started sometime, and sometime before the recorded history which it seems totally to pervade. But to postulate a chronological beginning of sin entails very little of what the doctrine of original sin has been thought to express. For initial sinfulness to take on any of the main connotations of original sinfulness, it must be linked to subsequent sinfulness not only in temporal succession, but in some kind of causal sequence.

It is that linkage which modern writers have thought to include in their conceptions of the "sin of the world," first widely popularized in the book *Man and Sin* by Piet Schoonenberg, who has developed and in some respects altered its ideas in a number of subsequent publications. What the phrase most basically represents in these writings is the entire history of human sinfulness, from its first appearance throughout all its subsequent realizations. Each human individual born into the world is by that very fact inserted into that history. Therefore all earthly human existence is unavoidably situated in a sinful environment. But the boundaries between self and environment are notoriously permeable. We are essentially social beings even when we are unsociable beings, and the social currents of our milieu flow through us as well as around us. What we are humanly includes what we become socially, and what we become socially is greatly determined by what our social situation already is. These are considerations to which modern philosophy has been extremely sensitive and for which modern social sciences have furnished overwhelming corroboration. And to the extent that one holds them as convictions, it becomes clear that the sequence of human sinning, as a component of that human social history in which all our lives are situated and all our cultures formed, cannot be a merely numerical and chronological sequence, and must be a chain, ramifying into an ever more complex network, of active influence.

It is not difficult to concede that this conception of the sin of the world gives an intelligible account of the historical continuity of human sinfulness. Some, indeed, have thought of it as including all that is clearly meaningful in the doctrine of original sin. A problem does arise, however, insofar as original sin is understood to be strictly universal. For there seems to be no obvious reason for denying that participation in the sin of the world might have at least temporary individual exceptions of a quite ordinary kind. Such would be the case of persons, such as infants, whose condition appears to make them simply incapable of the kinds of social and moral response that involvement in the world's sin would seem to presuppose.

It is in connection with this question of sin's universality that speculations about the sin of the world have been frequently linked to a quite different line of thought. Throughout the history of Christianity, the idea of sin has, of course, always been closely related to the idea of salvation in Jesus Christ. It has always been a central Christian affirmation that Christ is indispensable for human salvation. A number of modern writers are insistent that this idea be maintained as the starting point for reflections on sin, with the implication that what sin essentially means, in Christian thought, is humanity's need for salvation in Christ. This entails a quite different point of view from one that begins with an acknowledgement of sin as a perceived problem of human evil, and then acknowledges Christ as the revealed solution of that problem. In this perspective, the Christian occupies the position of one whose basic conviction is faith in the Gospel message of salvation in Christ, implying, of course, an antecedent need for that salvation. It is that need which is designated as sin. Conceived in this way, original sin precisely means the condition of humanity insofar as it lacks salvation in Christ. Sin is accordingly measured rather against that salvation to which it looks forward, than against a state of blessed innocence to which it looks back. What sin represents is, from this point of view, not the forfeiture of life's original quality, but the unaccomplishment of its ultimate destiny: not paradise lost, but, as it were, paradise ungained. Reinterpreted along these lines, it is evident that the doctrine of original sin becomes virtually detached from the doctrine of the fall. Somebody must, no doubt, have been the first human sinner or sinners, and he, she, or they must, at some point, have committed their first sin. But that is of little theoretical importance to exponents of the kind of theology we are now considering, some of whom prefer to apply the very name Adam to humanity as a whole insofar as it is not yet united with Christ and is, by that very fact, in a state of sin.

A further consequence of this kind of approach to the theology of original sin is that it eliminates the notion of humanity's having been reassigned by God a kind of substitute destiny, for the achievement of which the incarnation was the chosen means. In other words, there is not first a plan of creation, which is then foiled, and subsequently replaced by a kind of emergency plan of redemption. There is rather a single creative intention of God which includes, and indeed primarily envisages, the destining of humanity to salvation through union with the Word Incarnate. It has been understandably objected that it seems misleading to designate as sin what is described as a condition rather of uncompletedness than of malice or guilt. Some writers have accordingly preferred to restrict the term "sin" to a condition resulting from positively resisting or rejecting the salvation given in Christ.

More important than the varying details of these modern theologies of original sin is a common direction of thought whereby they diverge sharply from typical earlier accounts. Broadly speaking, what all of them involve is a tendency to regard basic human defectiveness as an unformed or underdeveloped, rather than a deformed or degenerate state. Accordingly, they situate human sinfulness within a process and understand it primarily with reference to the ultimate goal of that process. Human evil is thus measured in the first place as a distance between present unfulfillment and future fulfillment. Although this point of view is evidently congenial to biblical eschatology, it is not surprising that its prominence in modern thought belongs to a time when evolutionary conceptions have been influential in nearly every area of culture. Recent Catholic writings on this subject are strongly reminiscent of earlier trends in liberal Protestant thought that were closely related to an evolutionary world-view. Nevertheless, it has been correctly pointed out that history also provides much more ancient precedent for new directions of thought about original sin.

The most familiar understanding of original sin found in nearly

all the Christian Churches, and presupposed by a great many doctrinal formulations, is readily traceable to St. Augustine, and in particular to Augustine's controversy with Pelagianism. Most Christians
have taken this so much for granted that they may be quite surprised
to discover how little of this Augustine heritage is plainly discoverable
in the Bible. And readers of early Christian literature are likely to be
similarly surprised, not only by the inconspicuousness of ideas like
Augustine's, but also by the presence of interestingly different alternatives. Of these, the most fully developed example is furnished by
Irenaeus, who in the last quarter of the second century—just about
halfway from Paul to Augustine—was one of the first to issue a systematic resume of orthodox belief against the increasingly formidable
threats of heresy. One may, from reading different accounts of Irenaeus' teaching about the fall and original sin, form quite different
notions of what he actually had in mind, and that confusion is not fully
dispelled by a careful reading of his own writings. But for our purpose
it is sufficient to consider that interpretation of Irenaeus' thought
which has been increasingly favored by recent scholars and is considered by some of them to provide a basis in tradition for characteristically modern reinterpretations of original sin.

Irenaeus considers the biblical saying that man was created in
God's image and likeness to include two distinct assertions. Thus, likeness to God results from the outpouring of the Spirit, and what
humanity possesses apart from this is that image of God which is the
natural form of an intelligent human creature. But as the outpouring
of the Spirit is a process, the likeness to God which results from it
corresponds to a course of development or progressive growth. The
ultimate goal of that development is represented by the actual likeness
of God, his divine Son. Accordingly, for Irenaeus, Adam is not originally a kind of superman, fully perfected from the start. He is rather
a being possessed of God's image and destined to grow, by the Spirit's
outpouring, into that likeness of God which is the likeness of his Son.
The original human condition is thus appropriately likened to child-

hood, full of real but as yet undeveloped potentiality. It is consistent
with this conception that the fall is described by Irenaeus, in markedly
sympathetic terms, as the succumbing of an essentially naive and gul-
lible human creature to the wiles of diabolic temptation. The fall,
occasioned by this succumbing, is therefore not conceived as the sudden deterioration of a highly perfected human condition. It is rather
the curtailment of what should have been a process of spiritual
growth. Thus humanity's fallen state represents a kind of arrested
development.

The fall, as thus conceived by Irenaeus, does not represent a
definitive frustration of God's creative plan. Neither, therefore, does
redemption represent the bringing into play of an altogether different
divine plan. On the contrary, redemption is the effectuation, in view
of the fall and of human sinfulness, of God's original and permanently
valid plan for his human creation. The climactic realization of that
plan is what Irenaeus characteristically refers to as the recapitulation
of all things in Christ. Historically viewed, this recapitulation begins
with the incarnation, whereby the Son of God becomes a second
Adam who, as it were, reverses through his own history the process by
which the first Adam fell, and reestablishes the likeness of God in that
humanity of which he has become part.

It is clear enough why Irenaeus' account of the fall, as just out-
lined, should have attracted the interest of modern thinkers desirous
of interpreting original sin in the revisionist manner previously
described. For some of them it represents a respectable alternative,
within Christian tradition, to intransigent Augustinianism. Efforts
have accordingly been made to show that similar alternatives reappear
with significant frequency in the history of Christian theology,
although, especially in the West, they have been greatly eclipsed by
Augustine's immense authority. It must nevertheless be acknowledged
not only that Irenaeus' teaching is very obscure in some important
respects, but also that it does not begin to cope with the many problems that Augustine, for good or ill, took carefully into account. It

remains to be seen whether, in confrontation with similar problems, an Irenaean understanding of the fall can be maintained as consistently as an Augustinian one, while at the same time preserving its supposed congeniality to modern thought. In Irenaeus, modern speculation about original sin may find legitimate historical encouragement; it would be premature to suggest that it can find there substantial theological confirmation.

8
Mortal Sin, Venial Sin, and Fundamental Option

It has often been observed that modern thought, especially under the influence of modern psychology, inclines us to liken a human being to an onion—a thing of layers, to whose inner depths we gain access by peeling away successive surfaces. Although the distinctive modernity of this point of view is greatly exaggerated, for similar implications are discoverable throughout much of the history of human expression, recent thought has tended to apply it more systematically. And in Catholic moral theology it has acquired a rather sudden prominence, particularly with respect to the assessment of sin.

Nearly everyone does, at one time or another, relate specific instances of moral behavior to a kind of stratified conception of moral agency. How many parents, for example, have qualified their admission of even quite serious misbehavior on the part of one of their children by noting that he or she is, such offenses notwithstanding, "a basically good kid"? This conception of the basic goodness of a person, regarded as compatible with definite badness of the person's behavior, implies that the quality of an action does not necessarily reflect the basic quality of the agent. Since every action may be presumed to reflect some quality of its agent, it must be supposed in such cases to reflect something non-basic, or at least less basic than the goodness whose basic reality is affirmed. In like manner we often remark that the doer of some discreditable deed was "not quite himself" when he did it, implying that, although in one sense he certainly was the author of the deed, his action was not in direct or immediate continuity with his "real self." Similarly, we distinguish between performances that a performer has and those he has not "put himself into," and between expressions that are and others that are not "deeply intended." In all such turns of phrase a distinction is implied between relatively total or central, and relatively partial or peripheral, origins of individual conduct. Thus, a person who is believed deeply to love another person, but who does some decidedly unloving thing to that other person, may reasonably claim that his deeply loving relationship was not thereby annihilated or shown to be unreal. In other words, it may be claimed that to be loving and to act unlovingly are not always mutually exclusive.

In cases like the one just cited, in which the moral badness of an act does not exclude reasonable belief in the contrary basic goodness of the agent, one may ask on what that reasonable belief is founded. Rather clearly, when it is reasonable it is normally founded on knowledge of a great many other acts whose consistent manifestation of a certain kind of moral goodness leads us to regard that kind of moral goodness as a basic attribute of the person who performs them. Thus the loving friend in whose loving friendliness one continues to believe, on reasonable grounds, despite some grave offense, must be one who has acted like a loving friend too often and too impressively for the significance of that record to be overthrown by an isolated, even though strong, piece of contradictory evidence. In the forming of such ordinary moral judgments, it is evidently a kind of informal statistical inference that one employs, much as one might do in concluding that the basic academic excellence of a student whose record abounds in honor grades is hardly to be challenged on the basis of an isolated failure.

The kind of thinking about basic qualities, especially moral qualities, that we have been describing, ordinary as it is and reasonable as it seems, has been thought to raise certain difficulties for traditional Roman Catholic theology of sin. For that theology slowly evolved and at last firmly established a much-emphasized distinction between two kinds of actual sin, called respectively mortal and venial. This distinction, which has greatly influenced pastoral activity, envisages two profoundly different kinds of morally defective human actions, one of which does and the other of which does not radically alienate the moral agent from God, extinguishing the life of grace and cancelling the destiny of eternal salvation. Thus, in the ordinary view of unsophisticated Catholic believers, a mortal sin is an act of immorality which, if unremitted before the time of one's death, leads inevitably to eternal damnation. The chilling reminder that "you can go to hell for one mortal sin" was, for a very long time, part of the basic homiletic repertoire of every Catholic priest. To know, therefore, whether or not one had in fact committed any mortal sins was a basic concern of conscientious Catholic believers.

To provide for this concern, Catholic moral theology provided a set of basic criteria for identifying mortal sins, described in typical catechesis as comprising three necessary and sufficient conditions: gravity of matter, sufficiency of reflection, and fullness of consent. The first factor is understood to be objective, and any immoral action involving grave matter is accordingly said to be an instance of objectively mortal sin. Gravity of matter refers to both the general seriousness of an obligation that has been violated and the specific extent to which it has been violated in a given case. A great deal of Roman Catholic moral theology has been devoted to measuring the relative seriousness of obligations and extent of violations, employing modes of thought familiar enough to legal reflection—as, for example, in discriminating between felonies and misdemeanors. Whether or not an objectively mortal sin is also subjectively mortal sin depends on whether or not there is sufficient reflection and full consent. Here, too, moral theologians have furnished guidelines for determining the concrete meaning of sufficiency and fullness, very much as similar guidelines have been developed for the judicial assessment of personal guilt. If an action is a mortal sin, both objectively and subjectively, it is understood to entail the catastrophic religious consequences already referred to, amounting to that spiritual death of estrangement from God and exclusion from salvation from which it derives its title as mortal, in the sense of lethal, sin.

It has seemed to a number of modern writers that this conception of mortal sin is difficult to reconcile with the plausible and common assumption previously discussed, namely that a person's basic moral goodness may persist even though he or she occasionally performs actions that are in sharp conflict with that moral goodness. For the prevailing understanding of mortal sin would seem to demand that if such moral lapses involved grave matter, sufficient reflection, and full consent, they must by that very fact abolish anything describable as basic goodness. Moreover, if one supposes, as a great many Catholics have supposed, that mortal sins may be committed very frequently, and coped with as they occur by frequent recourse to the sacrament of penance, we are forced to envisage in the course of ordinary human lives a sequence of relatively frequent and thoroughly abrupt transitions from basic holiness to basic sinfulness.

It is hard not to feel that there is something bathetic about this prospect of rapid fluctuation between the uttermost extremes of human moral and religious possibility. And it seems evident that a sense of that bathos has had much to do with recent interest in what are called fundamental freedom and fundamental option. What these terms refer to is the supposition of a basic moral quality or direction in an individual life which, being moral, reflects a freedom of self-determination. That is, a person may commit himself or herself to a whole order of values, and such a commitment may endure despite sporadic deviations. A life may follow a definite direction even though it does so somewhat erratically. To commit oneself in this way to the order of moral values that is essential to the Christian understanding of salvation is a basic exercise of freedom, a fundamental option. A contrary commitment, repudiating that order of values, is, of course, equally possible and equally basic. It is commonly supposed by modern theologians that Thomas Aquinas was correct in judging that, once moral maturity is reached, one or the other of these commitments must be made—that the fundamental option cannot be avoided or indefinitely postponed. It is likewise supposed that once such a choice is made it governs the basic course of one's moral life as long as it is not, at an equally basic level of free choice, actually contradicted, repudiated and replaced by an opposite decision that gives an opposite moral direction to life. It is these fundamentally different trends of moral existence, rooted in fundamentally opposed acts of self-determination, that represent for many modern theologians the proper reference of a distinction between a life of grace and the extinction of that life which is mortal sin. It is not denied that these fundamentally opposite trends can be reversed during the course of an individual's life. But it is denied that so profound a reversal can be satisfactorily identified with the simple performance, knowingly and willingly, of any of those actions traditionally classified as mortal sins. This has led some writers to recommend an additional distinction between serious sin, as involving grave matter, and mortal sin, as entailing the definitive rejection of a godly course of life. Presupposed in this distinction is the possibility of an individual's committing a serious sin without becoming, simply by that act, mortally sinful. Also presupposed by most advocates of the distinction is that to lapse into mortal sinfulness is a process, often subtle and protracted, of moral and religious self-subversion which may culminate in a particular infraction but which cannot be simply identified with it.

One obvious practical advantage of this way of thinking about mortal sin is that it places the sinfulness of omission on the same plane with the sinfulness of commission. It is not hard to see how a long-continued abstinence from acts of moral goodness might represent a profound reversal of moral life ultimately describable as mortal sinfulness. On the other hand, traditional ways of describing mortal sin as a specific violation made it very difficult to relate the idea of mortal sin generally entertained by Catholics to the kind of mortal sinfulness Jesus seems to have had in mind in his famous parable of the final judgment, where divine condemnation is pronounced against those who "did it not to one of the least of these" and thereby "did it not to me." To scrutinize one's conscience for mortal sin, as Catholics so often did, by a kind of tallying up of actions categorized as grave offenses can easily obscure the moral significance of even lifelong neglect of occasions for active goodness. When personal sinfulness is conceived as a record of violations, a career of selfish indifference can easily appear as a history of innocence.

It should be evident that the kind of theology we have been considering is not one that discards the idea of mortal sin. But it is one that makes it much easier to speak of a state called mortal sin or mortal sinfulness, than of isolated actions called mortal sins. Mortal sinfulness would, no doubt, have to be precipitated by some definite exercise of moral behavior, but the precipitating event might be rather inconspicuous to consciousness, and its result might be clearly discernible only long afterward, in the light of accumulated indications. Realistic as this may seem, however, it entails certain problems for Catholics. For Catholic sacramental theology and pastoral practice have to reckon with the teaching of the Council of Trent, requiring regular recourse to the sacrament of penance by anyone guilty of mortal sin, and further requiring that the penitent confess, according to their species and number, all the mortal sins he or she has committed since the last valid confession.

The classifying and numbering of mortal sins which is thereby enjoined, and which long remained a conspicuous feature of Catholic penitential piety, is clearly predicated on a conception of mortal sin that recent theology tends to discredit. A certain tension exists at present over whether the Tridentine doctrine should deter us from accepting these recent theological trends, or whether on the contrary such theological reconsiderations should alter our understanding and practical implementation of Trent. What this tension seems mainly to have conveyed to the non-theological public is a vague but strong sense that the Catholic understanding and obligation of confession is not what it used to be. Under the circumstances, it can hardly be surprising that sacramental confession has been widely abandoned, despite praise-worthy efforts to reestablish it on a sounder basis as an act of peniten-tial worship based on faith in the reconciling love of God.

Our discussion has presented the recently popular idea of a fun-damental option as referring to a basic personal commitment that gives a deep, prevailing moral direction to the exercise of freedom in an individual life. So profound an option, it was suggested, could not be made or reversed lightly, and therefore it is hardly conceivable that contrary fundamental options should succeed one another in anything like rapid succession. Nevertheless, contrary fundamental options evi-dently can succeed one another, and their sequence would, in the view of some modern theologians, correspond to the reality of transition between a state of sanctifying grace and a state of mortal sin. Relating this conception to the traditional Catholic understanding of individual eschatology, the ultimate fate of each individual must apparently depend on what fundamental option was in fact governing the basic course of one's moral life when that life was terminated by death. However, at this point modern speculations about the fundamental option have been complicated by other modern speculations, enter-tained in some cases by the same theologians, concerning what has come to be known as the final option.

In its most specialized usage, the final option means something over and above a chronologically last fundamental option which, because it would have determined a person's basic moral orientation at the time of death, must prove to be eschatologically decisive. Final option does not refer simply to the fundamental option that a person brings, as it were, to the occasion of his or her death. Rather it refers to an option in which self-determination supposedly enjoys perfect freedom, of which death itself is uniquely and invariably the occasion. Leading proponents of this idea have maintained that this final option takes place not before death, when freedom is still limited and personal destiny still undecided, nor after death, when personal destiny has already been irrevocably decided, but in or at death itself. Whether or not any coherent sense can be made of the supposed occurrence of a real human decision neither during life nor after death would seem to be a troublesome question. However, a number of modern theologians appear to be untroubled by it, and they dispose of the seeming dilemma by reference to a metaphysical moment or non-temporal transition in which (one could scarcely say during which) the final option takes place. Supposing, in deference to respected authors, that this is not logically meaningless, one must still deal with the further question of how such a final option is related to the other options, including the fundamental option or options, that have preceded it during life.

If the final option is a reality, and if it is morally ultimate and eschatologically decisive because accomplished in pure freedom, then it might seem as though no previous option, including fundamental options, could be ultimate or decisive. But in that case, developing the idea of fundamental option as a basis for reinterpreting the traditional concept of mortal sin would not seem very illuminating. For the final option would seem to represent the one and only occasion on which truly mortal sin could occur. And in that case the whole eschatological relevance of moral behavior during temporal life becomes very hard to comprehend. For a final option that was truly an exercise of unimpeded freedom could, as easily as not, reverse the direction of any and all previous moral determinations. Moreover, the kind of finality attributed to the final option would seem to imply that to exercise it wrongly (if one can even imagine its being exercised wrongly under the supposed conditions) would constitute a sin that was both strictly mortal and strictly unforgiveable. And indeed, the whole theology of divine grace as justifying sinners would seem to have no real applicability to ultimate human destiny. Evidently, a number of issues remain to be thought out more clearly before it can be plain that final option theories are reconcilable with faith—or, indeed, with reason.

9
Sin and Moral Theology

Roman Catholics are the only Christians who make familiar use of the phrase, which came into common academic use only after the Reformation, "moral theology." This does not of course mean that earlier Christians, or non-Catholic Christians, consider theology irrelevant to morals, or morals irrelevant to theology. Part of what it does mean is that Catholics have, in relatively modern times, distinctively separated moral questions from other theological concerns, and that they have developed a distinctive way of approaching the moral sphere. Such an approach has already been described as one characterized by a highly juridical form, greatly preoccupied with classifying types of sinful behavior and factors influencing degrees of guilt, and strongly oriented toward the practical solving of cases of conscience. It was noted that this form of moral theology was to a great extent dictated by the requirements of Roman Catholic theology and discipline of the sacrament of penance (or reconciliation). And it was also pointed out that this kind of moral theology both presupposes and fosters an understanding of sin in predominantly legal terms, as behavior in violation of divine laws.

Until less than a generation ago, and for several centuries, Catholic textbooks of moral theology, in both form and content, bore a close family resemblance to one another. The general order of their topics, logic of their arguments, and nature of their presuppositions were quite predictable. And, at least to the uninitiated, intellectual differences among them were likely to seem relatively trivial. Such uniformity was, in fact, cultivated and virtually enforced as part of an effort to determine centrally a standard curriculum of seminary studies. In relatively recent years, however, Roman Catholic moral theology has exhibited a variety of significant departures from this pattern shaped by confessional casuistry. In fact, the recently familiar genre is already almost extinct, the old books being little used, and new ones of the same type being rarely published. Moral theology continues, of course, to be written, but its recent literature has assumed no uniform pattern, representing a growing variety of perspectives, emphases, and methodologies. At the same time, moral theology remains influential in Catholic popular and academic culture and has decided influence on what is being said and thought about sin.

One of the earliest of the modern departures in moral theology was originally closely linked with renewed interest in the writings of St. Thomas Aquinas, and it continues to be a vigorous trend, though with greatly diminished Thomistic emphasis. Thomas Aquinas, it may be recalled, organized the greater part of what would later be thought of as the subject matter of moral theology in relation to two sets of virtues: the four so-called cardinal virtues of prudence, justice, temperance, and fortitude, and the three so-called theological virtues of faith, hope, and charity. It would take us far beyond the scope of this book to examine this system in detail, but it has an obvious and important general implication for thinking about sin. General conceptions of sin, on a religious and theological plane, inevitably reflect general conceptions of immorality on a secular and philosophical plane. If morality is thought of primarily in terms of virtue, immorality must be thought of primarily in terms of vice, and thoughts about sin will be modified accordingly.

Virtues and vices are not acts. According to a classical tradition they are better thought of as habits, that is, as psychological attitudes and aptitudes disposing the persons who possess them to behave in certain ways. Thus when we say someone has the vice called cowardice, we mean that he or she seems habitually disposed to avoid even those risks we believe good people ought to take. That is, we think of cowardice, like other vices, as a trait of character which finds expression in reprehensible behavior. Vices refer to ways people habitually are, as evidenced by ways they habitually act. Vices are not, of course, visible; they are inferred from patterns of visible behavior. But they are thought of as representing an intrinsic moral condition that is more basic than outward acts. Translating vice into religious language, sin is thought of in the first place not as a forbidden deed, but as a defective condition of one's moral being. Thus understood, sins, as isolated actions, are attributed to sin, as a persistent state. The primary sense of sin might thus be expressed less ambiguously as sinfulness. It is the way a sinner is, which accounts for the way a sinner behaves. And it is to this intrinsic, underlying factor that the term "sin" is primarily referred. Sin is thought of only secondarily as an overt instance of ethical misbehavior; more fundamentally it is thought of as an acquired defect of moral character. Such a defect is acquired, of course, by sinning, and there is a reciprocal relationship between the outwardly sinful acts and the inwardly sinful state.

The ethical merits of this approach are debated, but they are not at issue here. Our concern is with how this approach, once adopted, tends to affect the way one thinks about sin. And in this regard, it is clearly an approach that directs attention away from the particular moments in which transgressions are committed to a general course of behavior over a period of time. Character cannot be perceived in a momentary act; it can only be inferred from continued acquaintance with how a life is being led. To estimate a person's character we must be in touch with his or her biography. Accordingly, sin, likened to vice, assumes a distinctively historical, narrative dimension. It is seen as part of a story. And since the story must be conceived, if it exhibits virtue or vice, as narrating occasions of moral improvement or decline, it has to be read as an account of development. And if that is to make any sense, one must relate the story to some kind of goal. That is, the real story must be implicitly related to an ideal story in order to have any basis for judging whether what it manifests is growth or decline. It appears, therefore, that conceiving sin after the manner of vice leads naturally to conceiving it as an aspect not simply of human being, but of human becoming, or, in a popular phrase, of human fulfillment. Sinfulness thus comes to be regarded as a trend or phase of retrogression, deviation, or stagnation, a departure from or interruption of progress toward a developmental goal. This way of thinking certainly does not exclude reference to rules or laws of conduct, but it tends to understand such norms as guidelines for the progress of a human life toward its proper goal.

More or less simultaneously with moral theology's renewal of interest in the basic importance of virtue and vice, it has been challenged and modified by the school of thought which, in its more extreme formulations, has been labeled "situation ethics." Insofar as this approach has, in a qualified form, found a place in moral theology, it has had the effect of emphasizing the essential uniqueness of those circumstances which influence any given moral decision, and the limited adequacy of any normative formulation to make proper allowances for all morally relevant circumstances. Thus, situation ethics has been perceived as challenging the claims to absoluteness of any particular moral rules, and as representing such rules rather as useful general maxims than as strictly inviolable regulations. As one reads the cases cited by situation ethicists to support their position, it becomes clear that what are usually taken to be the decisive circumstances for making moral decisions and applying moral norms are the foreseen consequences of alternative courses of action. Thus, the hard cases cited tend to be those in which non-conformity with traditional norms promises to result in a much better balance of good over bad consequences than would conformity with them. With due reservations, more and more moral theologians have shown willingness to be described as consequentialists, that is, as persons who judge what ought to be done in large measure by what is likely to result.

Although it might seem possible to bring consequentialism into harmony with an emphasis on virtue and vice, by regarding those modifications of moral character as major consequences of ethical choices, most consequentialists attend chiefly to consequences of a more external and objective kind. Nor is this unreasonable, since whereas the presence of virtue and vice can only be inferred from the frequency of right and wrong conduct, the consequentialists think that the rightness or wrongness of conduct is mainly indicated by more directly verifiable results.

Consequentialism, therefore, fosters a conception of sin rather as exterior action than as interior disposition, and specifically as exterior action that results in more predominance of harm over benefit than would result from other possible exterior actions. As popularly understood, this leads to a virtual equation of that which is sinful with that which is harmful, where the harm in question is thought of as objective and observable. What most people take this to mean is harm inflicted on other people. Thus it is commonly retorted to accusations that certain behavior is sinful because it violates traditional norms, that it cannot be sinful because it does not "hurt anybody." Such a retort may, of course, be very short-sighted even in terms of its own principles, but the point to be noted here is that what those principles entail is a consequentialist interpretation of sin.

This consequentialist view of sin has been reinforced by another recently popular theme, originally having little explicit association with consequentialism. That is the theme, inspired by New Testament teaching, that the whole divine law can be epitomized as a summons to love. To be sure, the primacy of love in moral theology can claim the most authoritative support from Christian tradition. Nevertheless, it is a phrase that can be variously interpreted and still more variously applied. Recently there has been a strong tendency to interpret it as meaning that one should always act as beneficially as possible. And that is often further interpreted to mean that one should act in such a way as to do the most possible good and the least possible harm to others under given circumstances. And that, of course, is virtually to identify the primacy of love in moral theology with the primacy of consequentialism in ethical methodology. Sin will accordingly mean a contradiction, or absence, or deficiency of love, which will be translated into practical terms by reference to consequentialist criteria.

Here, once again, it would be a deviation from the purpose of this book to enter upon an ethical critique of consequentialism. Properly or improperly, consequentialism of the sort just described has in fact taken deep root in contemporary moral theology and has had profound effects on what is being said and thought about sin. In addition to what has already been cited, evidence of this effect can be seen in the greatly decreased attention paid by most recent moral theologians to the once highly developed topic of interior sins, that is, those sins that do not cause obvious exterior harm but remain part of the inner life of their perpetrator. Jesus' insistence that the sinfulness of adultery is no more verified in the external act than in the private disposition of one who "looks lustfully on a woman" and commits "adultery with her in his heart" is not indefensible on consequentialist grounds. But its defense on those grounds is not obvious, easy, or often undertaken. To read traditional moral discourses on interior sins, and then seek their counterparts in modern literature, is to discover something important about what, broadly speaking, they are not saying about sin.

There are, to be sure, many other characteristically modern trends in moral theology than the two that have been here singled out. But these two trends are especially relevant to our subject matter. Both character-centered ethics and consequence-centered ethics are thriving in current thought. But they tend to thrive quite separately, and efforts to synthesize their respective viewpoints are seldom undertaken. They tend, as a result, to foster not only different, but divergent interpretations of sin. And of course, along with their influences, those of older approaches to moral theology, including the strongly juridical one previously referred to, continue to be exerted from less innovative sources. The present multiformity of moral theology has accordingly fostered a corresponding diversity, especially at the level of pastoral and popular thinking, of perspectives on sin. And the largely unreconciled state of this diversity generates more than a little confusion.

To say that moral theology is considerably responsible for this confusion is certainly not to say that it is blameworthy for it. Moral theology had, in fact, become a grievously doctrinaire and stagnant discipline before efforts at a major reform were launched, mainly around the middle of the present century. Those efforts have been, on the whole, successful, inasmuch as modern moral theologians bring to their work more than their predecesssors did of what other academic disciplines normally demand and respect: an abundance of relevant information, insistence on strong evidence and clear argument, openness to alternative viewpoints and hypotheses, and readiness to abandon or modify discredited opinions. The cultivation of such intellectual credentials after what, for this discipline, had been rather dark ages could hardly be expected to generate an immediate general consensus. Whenever a number of informed and intelligent people start thinking hard about complicated matters, their thoughts are bound to differ, diverge, and at least occasionally conflict. To the extent that they agree, it can be only through constructive mutual criticism of their independent thoughts, correcting, clarifying, complementing, and confirming one another's procedures and conclusions. Agreements reached in that way are always attained slowly and never attained perfectly. But with reasonable people they are the only sorts of agreement that carry authority. What moral theologians are saying about sin is certainly less unanimous than it used to be. But it is also better worth listening to. And the variety of perspectives on sin that it introduces is hardly greater or more complicated than that which finds expression in the Bible itself.

10
Sin and Social Structures

Most sinful behavior is social behavior in the sense that it does not begin and end in a single individual but produces effects in others. In fact, the consequentialist approach previously considered leads easily, though not inevitably, to practically equating sin with behavior that is avoidably hurtful to others. The hurts inflicted by sin are of many kinds, and sometimes they are very subtle and insidiously gradual. Even more subtle and gradual is the spread of the harm done by sin, beyond the person or persons to whom it is most obviously and immediately done, to others who might have been thought to lie outside its sphere of influence. The ultimate extent of the harm one person inflicts upon another is, no doubt, impossible to estimate, and in most cases it is probably greatly underestimated. The idea that "no man is an island" is hardly a new idea; indeed it was already old when that phrase was coined three centuries ago. Probably, however, it is an idea whose truth has become more obvious in recent times, if only because in most parts of the world human lives are being lived closer and closer together and in ever more complex interdependence.

In the early part of the present century, Catholic theology cultivated a special sensitivity to the social ramifications of sin. This was owing in considerable measure to intensified theological interest in what came to be known doctrinally as the mystical body of Christ. Inspired by several passages in the Pauline literature that liken the Christian community to an organic body, comprising interdependent members subordinated to their common Head, identified with Christ, this became a major theme of modern Catholic ecclesiology and an occasion for rediscovering similar directions of thought in patristic and medieval literature. Doctrinal implications of this theme were developed systematically in several directions and contributed greatly to recapturing a sense of the proper relationship between ecclesiology and liturgy. To a lesser degree, attention was paid to the "morality of the mystical body," as implying that, in the economy of grace, Christian morality could never be adequately conceived as a strictly individual matter. And St. Paul's reminder that "if one member suffers, all suffer together" was applied specifically to the idea that actual sin has consequences for the spiritual life not only of the individual transgressor, but of the whole spiritual organism, so to speak, of which he or she is a part. It has already been noted that a similar sensitivity to the effects of sin beyond its most obvious victims, upon the community at large, has been reinforced by improved understanding of that covenant theology which deepened biblical understanding of divine law, violated by human sin.

Attitudes toward the social ramifications of sin have also been influenced, in ways that are less general and more practical, by developments in sociology and social ethics. New perspectives in both theology and the social sciences brought the term "social sin" into Protestant usage during the last two centuries, and it was taken up in Catholic circles on broadly similar grounds. Social sin is not a very precise phrase, and, if examined in a very literal way, it can easily be made to seem either nonsensical or vague to the point of uselessness. Nevertheless, it does, in a somewhat rhetorical way, call attention to some important realities.

One of those realities may be suggested by recalling the analogy between sin and crime which, although it has been often abused, has its legitimate uses. The analogy derives, of course, from the idea that sin is a punishable violation of divine law and, as such, comparable to crime which is a punishable violation of human law. Most of the time, people think of crimes as acts whereby a criminal injures others through kinds of behavior that the law, foreseeing the social injuriousness of such behavior, has prohibited and penalized. In modern times, however, we have become unhappily familiar with the phrase "organized crime," referring to something by no means new in the world, but increasingly common and ominously growing. Organized crime is especially difficult to cope with, and at the same time especially necessary to cope with, because it represents something much more complex and much more powerful than individual cases of violating criminal laws. Nor is it as simple as the familiar case in which several persons collaborate in a particular criminal undertaking, as, for example, a group of assailants or a gang of thieves. Organized crime connotes a more stable, systematic, and extensive arrangement for cooperation in crime. It functions by many of the same systematic means that are employed by legitimate organizations, but in pursuit of illegitimate objectives. It works, most often, like big business, but its business is big crimes, and its operations are uninhibited by any legal obligations it can successfully evade. Naturally, all sorts of things may occur or exist within the workings of organized crime that, considered in isolation, are perfectly innocent. But they all belong to a structure that is designed for the efficient accomplishment of criminal purposes. To thwart those purposes, it is the structure itself that must be assailed, for that structure can continue to function even though its component parts, human or otherwise, have from time to time to be replaced. Moreover, organized crime may be assisted or sustained by many who are not part of its organization or devotees of its purposes, of which they may be even unaware, but whose own innocent purposes are in some way served by it. Thus, organized crime may pay fair rent to honest landlords for property indispensable to its criminal ambitions; it may support political candidates, not themselves in the least criminally inclined, but committed to policies that are incidentally very convenient for organized crime; it may lavish patronage on perfectly respectable religious and charitable institutions with a view to the security of public esteem.

Now, without straining the resources of an imperfect analogy, it is quite possible, from a religious point of view, to think of social sin as organized sin. That is, just as complex structural arrangements may facilitate and thereby greatly extend criminal behavior, they may do the same for sinful behavior, whether it happens to be criminal or not. This does not, of course, mean that any person or persons have ever set up an organization precisely for the sake of increasing the world's total amount of sin. Neither, for that matter, is organized crime established precisely to multiply crimes. Neither crimes nor sins are committed for their own sake; in the one case as in the other, any organizing is for the sake of gaining or increasing some human gratification that, in the circumstances, is to be sought by forbidden means—whether forbidden by the state's law or by God's.

When, for example, a very large and prosperous commercial company temporarily lowers the prices of a demanded commodity so as to annihilate those small competitors whose capital does not allow them to survive long without profits, it is unlikely to do so out of sheer malevolence; it does so to increase the wealth of its owners and their prospects for increasing it further. Such behavior may or may not be criminal, depending on the laws of the place where it occurs. But whether or not it happens to be criminal certainly does not determine whether or not it is, from an ethical viewpoint, wrong, or, from a religious viewpoint, sinful.

For the sake of illustration, let us assume the worst about our commercial example. Let us assume the company to be already very secure and its owners' profits to be very handsome. It has plenty, but it wants more. And it can get more by tactics that are ruinous to others, limited by their more modest means. If we likened the company to a human individual, we should almost certainly characterize such behavior as viciously cruel, indicative of the most appalling excesses of greed. From a Christian religious viewpoint, we should think of it as immensely sinful. But if, having reached such conclusions, we attempt to locate, as it were, the vice and sinfulness, where alone vice and sinfulness can be located, in free human wills, obvious difficulties arise. For a corporation is not a person, except by legal fiction, and it has no free will. It includes and involves many human persons, in diverse capacities, whose free wills affect its behavior through extremely complex interaction. Where are the cruel and greedy ones who should repent their mistreatment of others? No concrete answer to that question is likely to seem fully satisfactory. When social structures reach a certain level of complexity, moral responsibility is shared and diffused to a degree that defies analysis.

Let us turn from purely commercial to mainly political examples. There currently exist many nations, some of them ostentatiously claiming to be Christian and Catholic, in which the forces of government and even of law virtually enslave great numbers of citizens, leaving them economically resourceless and vulnerable to the most outrageous forms of exploitation as conditions of their very survival. The governing personnel of such nations come and go, peacefully or violently, but the processes remain substantially unaltered and their effects essentially unchanged. The structure and functioning of such government is often supported by interests whose power is virtually guaranteed by economic conditions deriving from centuries of progressive maldistribution. Political injustice and economic injustice are mutually reinforcing, and both operate through strong enduring structures. Injustice there surely is, and cruelty, and greed. The whole arrangement appears pervasively wicked. And yet no easy step can be taken from a general perception of sinfulness to an identification of particular sinners and particular sins. To say that the chief beneficiaries of such a system are by that very fact sinners may ease one's sense of moral indignation, but it is neither very helpful nor very fair. To have inherited great wealth in a traditionally plutocratic society is not to become, by that very fact, in any distinctive sense a sinner. To accept ordinary class privileges immemorially instituted in one's culture may not be moral heroism, but insofar as it is personal sin it is the kind of sin almost everyone, almost everywhere, almost incessantly commits. Few people are either ethical geniuses or moral heroes. Culturally they are not reformers but conformists. And to suppose they could on their own be anything else is to have learned little of this world's reality.

Ordinary people accept without qualms of conscience those good things that come their way by means that their culture assumes to be legitimate. The pampered rich are, in most cases, as dominated by the structures of their society as are the tormented poor, and for outsiders to hurl accusations against them as individuals is at best naiveté, at worst hypocrisy. Nevertheless, something is certainly wrong—terribly wrong, and surely, in the eyes of enlightened Christian faith, sinfully wrong. So, we have come to use phrases like social sin, and sinful societies, in such a way as neither to minimize what in God's sight is plainly evil, nor to exaggerate the responsibility for that evil of even those individuals who profit from it. No doubt, in the last analysis, much of the wickedness in bad societies had its beginnings in bad choices, made, foolishly or maliciously, by individual human beings. But that last analysis can hardly be completed by finite minds. And to carry it even a little way is to learn that many of the individual culprits, whose decisions still cause untold suffering, are themselves long since dead and gone. And as a result, much of what is meant by social sin cannot be satisfactorily disposed of by any simple change of heart and readiness to make amends for one's wrongdoing.

As regards the subject matter of this chapter, this book's task is embarrassingly easy, because it is exclusively theoretical. For, to indicate what they are saying about sin by calling some of it social sin is to take only a small and distant step toward indicating what they—or we—ought to be doing about it. To grasp the idea of social sin is among the prerequisites for understanding, from a religious perspective, an enormous practical problem. And understanding the problem is among the prerequisites for solving it. But actually solving it is a task difficult even to begin, more difficult to continue, and plainly impossible ever to complete.

What reflections on social sin have mainly contributed to practical reform is a deepened awareness by Christians that effective measures must address themselves, beyond individuals and individual practices, to cultural mores, social structures, and collective policies. Participants in social sin, which all of us are in some degree, can only bring forth "fruit worthy of repentance" to the extent that they strive collectively so to alter the structures of their societies that systematic inequities are systematically reduced and compensated.

At this point it seems necessary to make the observation, admittedly trite but not intentionally supercilious, that if, from Christian motives, one wishes to do anything effectively about social sin, one had better know something about societies, how they are put together and how they work. And what that means is knowing a reasonable amount about what are currently termed the social sciences. Wishing to suggest, for example, how commerce and politics can be made less sinful departments of life while unwilling to learn the elementary lessons of economics and political science is unrealistic. It has been often noted that Christianity's deepest inquiries into the workings of individual morality exhibited the greatest attention to findings and theories of individual psychology. It is now, though only gradually, being realized that, by the same token, inquiries into the moral workings of societies cannot dispense with serious education in the social sciences.

11
Sin and Reconciliation—An Epilogue

In the preceding pages, reference has often been made to the renaming of penance as the sacrament of reconciliation. That change of terminology corresponds to a deepened and intensified awareness of the meaning and importance of reconciliation as the Christian remedy for sin. The idea that this term represents has, in fact, fair claim to be called the central idea of Christian theology. The same idea can, of course, be expressed by other language, and, as it happens, biblical vocabulary that is rendered most literally by terms of reconciliation is used rather sparingly and concentrated in the Pauline literature. Nevertheless, a review of that vocabulary in its several contexts provides a singularly illuminating way of introducing the idea and bringing its practical meaning into focus.

All of the New Testament words that we translate into English by terms of reconciling and reconciliation derive from a verb *(allassein)* meaning to change. This terminology is used in secular writings for both making one thing physically into something else, and exchanging, as in trade, one thing for another. That general usage, applicable to material things, has also a special application to relationships among persons. It is this latter application that became the basis of its Christian theological meaning. For one kind of change this terminology was popularly used to express was the changing of a negative personal relationship into a positive one, and in particular the changing of hostility into friendship.

We find one non-theological example in the New Testament where St. Paul, discussing the implications of Jesus' prohibition of divorce, calls upon a woman who has abandoned her spouse to either remain unmarried or else "be reconciled to her husband" (1 Cor 7:11). Although the expression "be reconciled" is grammatically passive, it is also imperative, and calls for a decidedly active initiative on the woman's part. She is being asked to put her broken marriage back together. Her husband must, of course, cooperate in this, but the assumption of the case is that she rather than he was responsible for the rift, and therefore she, not he, must undertake to repair it.

This is very similar to the usage of that passage in the Sermon on the Mount which tells one who, when offering a gift at the altar, remembers that his brother has something against him, to "first be reconciled" (Mt 5:24), and only after that to offer the gift. Here again, the expression, grammatically passive, enjoins an action which depends for its success on the responsiveness of the offended party.

Another example of non-theological usage occurs in the preaching of the first Christian martyr, Stephen, when he recalls Moses' effort to "reconcile" his quarreling fellow Hebrews with the words, "You are brethren; why do you wrong each other?" (Acts 7:26). In all these instances the point to be noticed is that reconciliation presupposes alienation or enmity between persons and seeks to restore intimacy and friendship. It is on the foundation of this meaning that the theological understanding of reconciliation rests.

The New Testament teaching that deals explicit with reconciliation is concentrated in four passages of the Pauline writings. In the first of them, Paul, having proclaimed that Jesus' death and resurrection bring about a new human and even universal creation, goes on to say:

All this is from God, who through Christ reconciled us to himself and gave us the ministry of reconciliation; that is,

God was in Christ, reconciling the world to himself, not
counting their trespasses against them, and entrusting to us
the message of reconciliation. . . . We beseech you on behalf
of Christ, be reconciled to God (2 Cor 5:18–20).

Several points are noteworthy in this passage. First, the act of
reconciliation is attributed to God alone. Second, God reconciles
through and in Christ. Third, God reconciles to himself. Fourth, those
whom God reconciles are Paul and his fellow Christians, but, more
generally, the world. Fifth, those who have been reconciled are now in
the service of reconciliation, spokesmen for Christ, calling others to be
reconciled to God.

The next passage, in a constructive order, is the following:

For if while we were enemies we were reconciled to God by
the death of his Son, much more, now that we are reconciled,
shall we be saved by his life. Not only so, but we also rejoice
in God through our Lord Jesus Christ, through whom we
have now received our reconciliation (Rom 5:10–11).

Here three elements may be added to our findings from the preceding passage. First, our condition prior to reconciliation is described
as enmity. Second, our reconciliation through Christ is said to be
through his death as Son of God. And third, the reconciliation already
achieved through his death is distinguished from a salvation, by his
life, which is confidently anticipated.

The idea of reconciliation is further illuminated by a later passage, referring to Christ and addressed to Gentiles:

But now in Christ Jesus you who once were far off have been
brought near in the blood of Christ. For he is our peace, who
has made us both one, and has broken down the dividing
wall of hostility, by abolishing in his flesh the law of com-
mandments and ordinances, that he might create in himself

one new man in place of the two, so making peace, and
might reconcile us both to God in one body through the
cross, thereby bringing the hostility to an end (Eph 2:13–
16).

An important new perspective is here introduced regarding
Christ's significance for the relationship between Jews and Gentiles.
Jesus Christ is identified as "our peace," and that title is related to the
belief that he made peace by replacing with unity the inveterate
enmity of the two groups. In reconciling both of them to God, he oblit-
erates their difference, uniting them organically in a renewed humanity. Here "vertical" reconciliation seems to entail "horizontal" reconciliation; the reconciling of mankind to God and the uniting of Jews
with Gentiles are aspects of a single reality, called simply "peace,"
accomplished by God in Jesus Christ. This is a much more developed
statement of the idea that appeared earlier in Paul's reflection on the
fate of the Jews (Rom 11:15).

In the final passage to be considered, the initial reference is to
Christ, who has been just previously referred to as the Son and image
of God:

For in him all the fullness of God was pleased to dwell, and
through him to reconcile to himself all things, whether on
earth or in heaven, making peace by the blood of the cross.
And you, who once were estranged and hostile in mind,
doing evil deeds, he has now reconciled in his body of flesh
by his death, in order to present you holy and blameless and
irreproachable before him (Col 1:19–22).

In this passage the object of reconciliation is described in terms
of remarkably sweeping universality. What God has reconciled is "all
things, whether on earth or in heaven." A further implication of what
reconciliation means is brought out in the concluding verse, where reconciliation is conceived as preliminary to or preparatory for the pre-

sentation to God and by God of a mankind wholly purified and sanctified. The terms in which this latter idea is expressed are clearly borrowed from the language of sacrifice.

To review these passages, which together comprise the New Testament's explicit teaching about reconciliation, is to discover that, few and brief though they are, they are remarkably rich in theological content. A somewhat organized impression of their collective significance can be obtained by asking a series of questions whose answers they most obviously provide: Who reconciles? By what means is reconciliation accomplished? Who is reconciled? To whom is reconciliation directed? What does reconciliation presuppose? What does reconciliation effect? And, what lies beyond reconciliation?

Who reconciles? Clearly, God. God is always referred to as the subject, and never as the object of reconciliation. In other words, God is repeatedly said to reconcile, but he is never said to be reconciled. In the matter of reconciliation, God is conceived invariably as active, never as passive.

We ask by what means is reconciliation accomplished. And repeatedly, in every passage, the means, or medium, or instrument of reconciliation is identified with Jesus Christ, so that God reconciles "through Christ" and "in Christ" and "in union with Jesus Christ." But, more specifically, reconciliation, or its effect, is said to be "through the death of his Son," "through the shedding of his blood," "through the cross." To our question, therefore, about the means of reconciliation, we have both the general answer, Jesus Christ, and the more specific answer, Christ's death upon the cross.

The third question, concerning the object of reconciliation, is given an answer of ever-widening compass. In the earlier texts the object of reconciliation is successively identified with Paul and his fellow Christians, with the communities they evangelize, and with the Gentile and Jewish peoples as a whole. In the later texts, this expanding circle takes in "all things, whether on earth or in heaven."

The fourth question, to whom reconciliation is directed, has the same answer as the first—God alone. As it is from God that all rec-

Sin and Reconciliation

onciliation comes, so also it is to God that all reconciliation leads. But there is also a further implication in that the reconciliation of Jews and Gentiles to God entails their union to one another. The implication here that reconciliation has two interrelated dimensions is reinforced by the answer to the next question.

When we ask what change reconciliation effects, the answer is clear and uniform. In reconciliation, as in every change, something ceases to be and something else comes to be. In reconciliation, what ceases to be is called enmity; what comes to be is called peace. We note that the enmity referred to is mainly between humanity and God, but also between Jews and Gentiles, and in both cases reconciliation means the replacement of enmity by peace.

With regard to the last question, one cannot fail to notice that reconciliation is not referred to in terms of utter finality. Reconciliation is not the end of the story, but points beyond itself. Ultimately, what it points to is described as salvation and sanctification. But more immediately, it points to a task, a work to be undertaken in the service of its own furtherance. The reconciled are entrusted with the message, the ambassadorial mission, of reconciliation. What they have received, they are to transmit.

If we attempt to turn this set of theological abstractions into a more concrete analogy, a rather definite picture, at least in its main outlines, emerges. It is a picture which represents humanity as having rejected God, making humanity God's enemy. But it is likewise a picture which represents God as not having rejected humanity, as not having made himself humanity's enemy. It is furthermore a picture which represents the death of Jesus Christ as a divine instrument for turning back toward God a humanity which had turned away from him. It is a picture which represents this being turned back toward God as entailing a participation in the very instrumentality that brings it about. And finally it is a picture which represents this turning back toward God as a reestablishment of peace, which is humanity's right relationship to God, and the basis of all right relationships throughout human society and the whole created universe.

In choosing to end this very modest account of what I think "they are saying about sin" with a biblical reconstruction of what I think they are saying about reconciliation, I have not intended a digression, but a summation that is also a transition. For what Christians as such say about anything can claim only as much original validity as it has valid relationship to the Gospel. Aside from that, Christians cannot know more about the phenomenon of sin, objective or subjective, than anybody else. The "sin of the world," with all its components, is only what every thoughtful dweller in the world comes to know all too familiarly. What Christians claim they also know is the one "who takes away the sin of the world," and something of what it means, and how it feels, for him to take away that sin. They claim no more (or less) acquaintance than others with the world's sickness, but they do claim more acquaintance with its cure and with the convalescence that is wrought by it. Christian wisdom has nothing to add to what has been well called "the banality of evil," but it does have something to add to what we may be tempted to call the anomaly of good. And that is why this brief concluding summary of a biblical theology of reconciliation ought to be a transitional chapter, whose sequel volume might well be entitled, "What Are They Saying About Peace?"

Suggestions for Further Reading

G. C. Berkouwer, *Sin* (Grand Rapids: Eerdmans, 1971)

Franz Böckle, *Fundamental Moral Theology* (N.Y.: Pueblo, 1980)

Emil Brunner, *Man in Revolt* (London: Lutterworth, 1939)

Bernard Cooke, *Ministry to Word and Sacraments* (Philadelphia: Fortress, 1975)

A. M. Dubarle, *The Biblical Doctrine of Original Sin* (N.Y.: Herder, 1964)

Sean Fagan, *Has Sin Changed?* (Garden City: Doubleday, 1979)

Henry Fairlie, *The Seven Deadly Sins Today* (Washington, D.C.: New Republic, 1978)

Nels Ferré, *Evil and the Christian Faith* (N.Y.: Harper, 1947)

A. Gelin and A. Descamps, *Sin in the Bible* (N.Y.: Desclee, 1964)

Andrew M. Greeley, *The New Agenda* (Garden City: Doubleday, 1975)

Tad Guzie and John J. McIlhon, *The Forgiveness of Sin* (Chicago: Thomas More, 1979)

Bernard Häring, *Free and Faithful in Christ,* I (N.Y.: Seabury, 1978)

Bernard Häring, *Sin in the Secular Age* (Garden City: Doubleday, 1974)

Zachary Hayes, *What Are They Saying About Creation?* (Ramsey, N.J.: Paulist, 1980)

Eugene C. Kennedy, *A Sense of Life, A Sense of Sin* (Garden City: Doubleday, 1976)

Sharon MacIsaac, *Freud and Original Sin* (N.Y.: Paulist, 1974)

William E. May, ed., *Principles of Catholic Moral Life* (Chicago: Franciscan Herald, 1980)

John T. McNeill, *A History of the Cure of Souls* (N.Y.: Harper & Row, 1951)

Karl Menninger, *Whatever Became of Sin?* (N.Y.: Hawthorne, 1973)

Bernard Murchland, ed., *Sin* (N.Y.: Macmillan, 1962)

H. Richard Niebuhr, *The Kingdom of God in America* (N.Y.: Harper & Row, 1937)

Reinhold Niebuhr, *Moral Man and Immoral Society* (N.Y.: Scribners, 1960)

Reinhold Niebuhr, *The Nature and Destiny of Man* (N.Y.: Scribners, 1947)

Marc Oraison *et al., Sin* (N.Y.: Macmillan, 1962)

V. Palachovsky and C. Vogel, *Sin in the Orthodox Church and in the Protestant Churches* (N.Y.: Desclee, 1960)

P. Palazzini and S. Canals, *Sin, Its Reality and Nature* (Dublin: Sceptre, 1964)

Norman Pittenger, *Cosmic Love and Human Wrong* (N.Y.: Paulist, 1978)

Gottfried Quell *et al., Sin* ("Bible Key Words") (London: Adam & Charles Black, 1951)

Karl Rahner, *On the Theology of Death* (N.Y.: Herder, 1965)

Karl Rahner, *Theological Investigations, I* (Baltimore: Helicon, 1961)

Karl Rahner, *Theological Investigations, VI* (Baltimore: Helicon, 1969)

Karl Rahner, *Theological Investigations, XI* (Baltimore: Helicon, 1974)

J. Regnier, *What Is Sin?* (Westminster, Md.: Newman, 1961)

Paul Ricoeur, *Fallible Man* (Chicago: Regnery, 1965)

Paul Ricoeur, *The Symbolism of Evil* (Boston: Beacon, 1967)

Henri Rondet, *Original Sin: The Patristic and Theological Background* (N.Y.: Alba House, 1972)

Henri Rondet, *The Theology of Sin* (Notre Dame, Ind.: Fides, 1960)

Piet Schoonenberg, *Man and Sin* (Notre Dame, Ind.: University of Notre Dame Press, 1965)

Juan Luis Segundo, *Evolution and Guilt* (Maryknoll, N.Y.: Orbis, 1974)

Gerard S. Sloyan, *Is Christ the End of the Law?* (Philadelphia: Westminster, 1978)

H. Shelton Smith, *Changing Conceptions of Original Sin* (N.Y.: Scribners, 1955)

Michael J. Taylor, ed., *Mystery of Sin and Forgiveness* (N.Y.: Alba House, 1971)

F. R. Tennant, *The Origin and Propagation of Sin* (Darby, Pa.: Arden, 1980)

N. P. Williams, *The Ideas of the Fall and of Original Sin* (London: Longmans, 1929)